Not Dark Yet

Not Dark Yet

Mike Harfield

Foreword by
DAVID LLOYD

First Published 2008

Reprinted August 2008

Reprinted December 2008

Reprinted January 2009

Reprinted June 2009

Published by My Back Pages Publishing
55 Meadow Drive
Prestbury
Cheshire
SK10 4EY
www.mybackpages.co.uk

Realised by Loose Chippings Books
The Paddocks
Chipping Campden
Gloucestershire
GL55 6AU
www.loosechippings.org

Printed and bound by J F Print, Sparkford, England

ISBN 978-0-9554217-1-6

This book is about cricket and other stuff but mainly cricket. No names have been changed to protect either the guilty or the innocent.

Dedicated to my wife, my mother and Gary Sobers.

Contents

Foreword

Commentary boxes are great places to leave cricket books lying around. I took NOT DARK YET to Sri Lanka with me and did just that.

I also 'loaned' it to the great C.M.J. of T.M.S. He offered that it was 'very entertaining and enjoyable'. That, of course, is C.M.J. speak. I nearly wet myself......which is my speak. In fact I laughed so much I nearly passed my fags round! Sorry, in these days of political correctness I should add a rider here that SMOKING KILLS AND MAKES YOU WHEEZE A LOT.

Lots of my mates get a mention in the book and Robert George Dylan Willis will be immensely proud of the chapter titles. Big Bad Bob, 'Towser' Andy Lloyd, myself and a few of our non-cricket mates would be perfect for this fixture........not for the cricket aspect, you understand. No, we get very enthusiastic after stumps!

I even read passages of NOT DARK YET to a colleague of mine in the commentary box who features from time to time in the book. As he has recently been made a Knight of the realm, he denies all knowledge of any reference to him in ANY book...... but I can reveal he did have a chuckle about the time........... read on!

David Lloyd

Lancashire, England & Sky commentator

1. Tomorrow Is A Long Time

It was the 1st May 1976. Colin, Roger and I were trying to decide what to do with the rest of our lives and, more particularly, what to do at the weekends. Sitting in a pub drinking Fullers ESB, waiting for the FA Cup Final to start, is a great way to do this.

In those days, most pubs didn't have TVs so it was back to someone's flat with a couple of cans to see the match. The thing about Fullers ESB is that if you have too many pints (i.e. more than three) you can barely remember what you discussed, what the score was or sometimes even who was playing. (Southampton 1 Manchester United 0, Bobby Stokes in the 83rd minute).

The next day we checked the papers to see if Southampton really had beaten Manchester United and then we returned to our earlier discussions. We had tried to analyse exactly what we did do at weekends and had struggled to come up with any meaningful answers. Looking back now, drinking all day and watching a football match on TV in the middle of the afternoon was a bit of a clue but probably too obvious then. We were in our mid 20s - before wives, children, mortgages, dodgy knees and bad backs. We all loved cricket but perversely had not played since school. There seemed no reason not to start playing again and so the idea of the Clifton Hampden match was conceived.

The plan was to get a team of friends together and play the Oxfordshire village where my parents lived. Clifton Hampden had a league side on Saturdays and played a few games on Sunday, including one against a Lord Gnome's XI, a team from Private Eye. Clifton Hampden was, and still is, a small village on the Thames, had a lovely cricket ground and two pubs. One was the Barley Mow which first opened 650 years ago and gets a mention in Jerome K. Jerome's novel 'Three Men in a Boat'. The other was the Plough, situated conveniently close to the cricket ground. What could be better? Contact was made and the club said that they would be delighted to entertain us.

As I like organising things and, more importantly, nobody else wanted to do it, I was designated captain. What could be difficult about getting eleven people together to play a friendly game of cricket? We were at the beginning of what was to become the hottest summer since records began. A weekend in Oxfordshire was on offer. Once I started asking around, and the word spread, my biggest problem would probably be choosing the best eleven players.

I managed to sign up Alan, a hockey player, Nick a

squash player, Rob a rugby player and Steve who was a footballer. You may notice a bit of a theme here. None of them actually played cricket. Never mind, at least they were keen to play and reasonably fit. I also recruited Hugh who I knew had played cricket because I had seen him do it at school. I had high hopes too for Ken who I worked with. He was a bit older than the rest of us; in fact he was really old - about 35. His unique attraction to me was that in his late teens, he had opened the innings for Blackpool in the Northern League with Rohan Kanhai. He had been a schoolboy hero of mine (Kanhai not Ken) and Ken had regaled me with many stories of Kanhai's prodigious batting and drinking skills. My thinking was that anyone who had batted with such a legend must be at least a half-decent player.

Unfortunately, Ken had given up cricket and taken up golf. I tried to goad him with what Colin Ingelby-Mackenzie, the Hampshire captain, had said. 'Golf is a game to be played between cricket and death' but to no avail. I also asked him for Kanhai's telephone number but that wasn't forthcoming either. Ken isn't dead yet and is still playing golf but he never did make it to any of the Clifton Hampden matches.

Time was marching on and I was beginning to get an inkling of the particular difficulties involved with trying to raise a cricket team. A week to go and, including Colin and Roger, I only had eight players. People I approached broadly fell into three categories:

1. They liked the idea of the river, the pubs and chatting with old friends in the sunshine but did not want to have a hard ball thrown or hit at them.

2. They really, really wanted to play but unfortunately had to visit their aunt/mark some homework/wash their hair.
3. They would like to play but would have to let me know later.

Over the years, I would become very familiar with all three categories. I had no problem with the first; it was going to be a social occasion and the more spectators the better. No problem with the second category either unless they happened to be a decent player in which case I was seriously upset. It was the third category that presented the main problem back in 1976 and continues to this day.

If he's more Johann Strauss than Andrew Strauss then there is no real difficulty; I just say I will get back to him. But if he's a good player, how long do you wait for him to commit and at what point do you say to the really keen guy who can't bat, bowl or field but has an attractive sister/wife/daughter and you know will definitely turn up - 'you're in'?

Captaining a cricket team is the hardest job in sport. If the team is doing well and wins easily, anyone could have done it. If the team is doing badly and loses, it is almost certainly the captain's fault. Everyone who plays cricket, and quite a few who don't, can point out what a captain is doing wrong and how he or she would have done it differently i.e. better. 'Infamy! Infamy! They've all got it in for me.' Kenneth Williams could well have been talking about the trials and tribulations of being a cricket captain.

Before you even get on to the pitch you have to get eleven players to agree to play. Then you have to hope and pray that they actually turn up. Some years later, Clive (an unreliable regular by then) assured me on the Thursday before a match that he would be at the pub on Sunday, well in time for the game. On Sunday morning he rang me. The conversation went something like this:

Clive: 'Hi Mike, it's Clive.'
Me, with a slow feeling of dread: ' Hi Clive.'
Clive: 'What's the weather like?'
Me: 'Fine, the sun's shining.'
Clive: ' It's raining here.'
Me: 'It's not raining here.'
Clive: 'So is the game on?'
Me, with a greater feeling of dread: 'Yes, definitely.'
Clive: 'It's really pouring here.'
Me, beginning to accept the inevitable: 'It's great here, the sun is shining.'
Clive: 'What time do we start?'
Me: '2.30, just like the last fifteen years.'
Clive: 'I'll see you soon then.'
Me: 'Looking forward to it.'

Clive never did make it that year and Richard, Ray's 12 year old son, on stand-by from the moment Clive rang, made his debut a couple of years earlier than perhaps he would have expected.

International captains don't have these concerns although player's paternity leave seems to be a new and growing problem. I can't remember this being an issue in the past. Can you imagine it? Botham to Brearley - 'sorry Skip, won't be able to make Headingley, Kath's expecting any day now'. Or Trueman to Dexter - 'I know I'm on 299 Test wickets but the wife wants me to be at the birth.'

Of my own three children, one was born just before the cricket season started, one after it finished and one inexplicably right in the middle of the season, and on a Saturday too! I was playing 2nd XI club cricket by then (i.e. the club had two XIs and I was in the 2nd one) and had to miss the match. Actually, I could have played if we had fielded first and I had opened the innings when we batted after tea, hit a quick-fire 50 and then raced to the hospital, which was only 10 miles away. There were too many uncertainties with this scenario, as anyone who has seen me bat would know, and sometimes you just have to put your wife and family first.

We did go and watch the game though. I thought it would be relaxing for Jill and it was a really important league match. The game was quite exciting and I thought Jill was enjoying it too. In fact she was having contractions and we only just made it to the hospital in time. Perhaps subconsciously, I wanted the baby to be born at the ground surrounded by cricket paraphernalia? What a delivery that would have been!

The baby was christened David, after David Gower, although if my wife ever reads this, it will be the first time she realises it. Well, it was 1985 and he had just scored 166 against the Australians in the 3rd Test and went on to score 215 in the 5th and 157 in the 6th. It was probably just as well that I didn't push my luck and suggest his middle name as well. David Ivon? That could have been terrible.

I suppose with Test cricket being more or less all the year round, it presents a bit of a problem for today's new men. I know that being at the birth of your child is a moving experience but does it really compare with hitting Glenn McGrath over his head for a boundary?

Back in 1976, I still only had eight players and it was the Wednesday before the game. Another work colleague was in the 'I'll let you know' category. Ray certainly talked a good game and, apart from being a Manchester City supporter, seemed a sound sort. I approached him again and secured his commitment. It turned out to be one of my best signings. Not only are we still good friends (he is godfather to the son inconveniently born in July) but in time he produced a son of his own (Richard, Clive's replacement). Richard turned into a decent player himself (better than his father anyway) and has played half a dozen times in the Clifton Hampden match.

That made nine. Increasingly frantic phone calls on Thursday and Friday secured the services of two 'friends of friends' and although I had never met them, I was assured that they would turn up. I was a naive and innocent cricket captain in those days and just assumed that they would.

2. All I Really Want To Do

The great thing about the Clifton Hampden match these days is that wives and children are an integral part of the occasion. The great thing about the Clifton Hampden match when it first started was that there were no wives and children. Yes, there were a few girlfriends, some of whom became wives in the fullness of time, although not necessarily to the person they were with at that first match; but crucially there were no children.

Please don't misunderstand me. Children are wonderful, but young children tend to put the kibosh on most of the things you enjoyed doing before you had them. Once they get to about 10, they don't need keeping an eye on all the time and become potentially useful. They can do the scoring, they can help look for balls hit into the cornfield by the opposition and they can be asked to play in an emergency. Indeed, from mid-teens onwards they will probably score more runs than their fathers and are definitely less likely to pull a hamstring while fielding.

Back in our salad days, pre-children, most of us met in Oxford on the Saturday, had a few drinks, strolled by the river, sometimes went for a punt (the one involving a long pole not a betting shop) and generally had a good time. We would then descend on Clifton Hampden and try to find somewhere to sleep for the night. I had a distinct advantage as I could sleep at my parents' house; others had to be more creative. That first weekend in 1976, I had to stop my father ringing the police when he saw a number of strange looking people rampaging around his garden. I explained that they were my friends and, after he had got over the shock, he welcomed them and actually grew to like some of them as the years went by.

This was before most of the team could really afford hotels, some still can't, so that year there were four tents and a Harley Davidson parked on the back lawn. Looking back now, my father, a keen gardener, took it rather well.

The Plough, one of the two pubs in Clifton Hampden, was about 200 yards from my parents' house and 400 yards from the cricket ground. It seemed the obvious place for a pre-match team talk. In those days, Ken and Beryl ran the Plough. Smoking was more or less compulsory, new customers were viewed with weary suspicion and the introduction of the sale of crisps was seen as a major culinary breakthrough.

Although most of us hadn't played cricket since school, confidence was surprisingly high. Indeed, there seemed to be some sort of correlation between the number of pints of Ushers drunk and the size of our impending triumph. By the end of

Saturday evening there was little doubt that we were going to be victorious the next day.

We reconvened at the Plough for lunch on Sunday and I began what was to become an annual ritual of worrying if all the players who said that they would meet at the pub would actually turn up. Sunday lunch is always a convivial affair with the opportunity to meet friends you might not have seen since the previous year. Then I try to encourage everyone to get to the ground in good time for the 2.30 start. We have never started on time in over 30 years of playing. It's surprising how difficult it is sometimes to get people to move the 400 yards from a pub to a cricket ground. That first year, most of the players were quite keen but it has got progressively more difficult as the years have gone on.

At the ground, I introduced myself to the Clifton Hampden captain. He gave me an old fashioned look when I asked if it would be OK if we borrowed some of their kit, like for instance, bats, gloves, pads, a ball and maybe some wicketkeeping gloves. I could tell that he wasn't sure whether I was trying to con him by pretending we had no kit or we were just a bunch of losers. Time would tell.

They won the toss and decided to bat. The names of Cox-Rogers, Goes and Bowden were to become familiar over the years but they held no fear for us at the time. Surely our mix of youthful enthusiasm and innate natural ability would make up for the fact that we hadn't actually played for a few years (or ever in a couple of cases).

And so the imaginatively named Mike Harfield XI took the field for the first time. I would like to say that we were following in the naming traditions of T.N.Pearce's XI and Lavinia, Duchess of Norfolk's XI but the truth is we never got around to coming up with a witty and original name. Have you ever wondered who exactly is T.N.Pearce? No, me neither but he always seems to get damned good teams together. Also, if Lavinia really is the Duchess of Norfolk, why does she always play in Sussex? There are plenty of good cricketers in Norfolk; it just so happens that they are all called Edrich. A team once played made up entirely of Edrichs. The two most famous were Bill Edrich who opened for Middlesex and England with the incomparable Denis Compton and John Edrich who was playing for England that summer in 1976. Both batsmen you notice - very flat, the pitches in Norfolk.

Considering it was our first outing, we bowled and fielded pretty well. Rob, the rugby player and Steve, the footballer, proved to be useful bowlers and Hugh, playing largely from memory, did a job for the team. Clifton Hampden declared at 159 for 9 and we took tea, quietly confident that we would give them a good run for their money. At 16 for 3 we were slightly less confident and at 23 for 6 there was serious cause for concern. We were eventually all out for 32 and the records show that we contributed to our downfall with 3 stumpings, 2 LBWs and a run out.

We were embarrassed, Clifton Hampden were sympathetic. We had a 10 over 'beer match' and lost that as well, although we did manage to get more than 32. 'Funny old game cricket' and 'It's only a game' were heard on more than one occasion as we drowned our sorrows afterwards. Actually, there is nothing funny about being bowled out for 32 and it quite clearly isn't just a game. Pride, self respect and your batting average are all at stake.

Something had to be done, so I hesitatingly asked for a rematch the following year. Obviously seeing a chance to improve their averages, not to mention their bar takings, the captain agreed and the Clifton Hampden match was born.

3. Caribbean Wind

Although it had only been a 'friendly' match and everyone had had a good time, especially the Clifton Hampden bowlers, there was no getting away from the fact that a score of 32 was an embarrassment.

For the rest of the year, I was preoccupied with one simple thought. How could I get a 6' 6" West Indian into the side for next year's match? For some reason, whenever you see a West Indian in a cricket team that you are about to play, you automatically assume that he's a really good player. He will bowl like Malcolm Marshall and bat like Viv Richards. Or at the very least, bat like Malcolm Marshall and bowl like Viv Richards. There's no real logic to this. It's unreasonable to expect all West Indians to be good at cricket but logic goes out of the window when you see a West Indian in the opposition team.

This subconscious thought would have been reinforced in 1976 by the West Indian touring party. They trounced England 3-0 in the Test series and played 21 other first class matches of which they won 15. Holding and Roberts were lethal, while Greenidge and Fredricks were as exciting an opening pair as you can imagine.

Viv Richards was in his pomp and scored 829 runs in four Tests. He missed the 2nd Test through injury. I think he hurt his jaw laughing at Tony Greig's bowling. Richards played shots that lesser mortals could only dream of. He seemed to be able to deposit the ball over the midwicket boundary wherever the bowler pitched it. Next ball he would play a classically correct cover drive. He combined Freddie Flintoff's brutal strength with Michael Vaughan's elegant class. He had Kevin Pietersen's arrogance but was cool in a way that somehow Pietersen just isn't. Maybe it's in the first names? It has to be said that Isaac Vivian Alexander is a lot cooler than Kevin Peter, so Richards did have a bit of a head start.

My interest in, some would say obsession with, West Indian cricketers started much earlier than 1976. The West Indian team that toured England in 1963 was what first ignited my interest in cricket and the series that year lit a flame that I know will never be extinguished. Rather worryingly, I can reel off the names of the 1963 West Indian team but would struggle to name all the current West Indian team.

1. Conrad Hunte
2. Michael Carew
3. Rohan Kanhai
4. Basil Buthcher
5. Gary Sobers
6. Joe Solomon
7. Frank Worrell
8. Derek Murray
9. Wes Hall
10. Charlie Griffith
11. Lance Gibbs

Actually, I had to look up Conrad Hunte's opening partner because he had more than one (McMorris and Rodriguez also played), but the rest have stayed with me year after year. Fragmented memories from that time include Basil Butcher's underarm throws from the boundary, Kanhai's exuberant batting, Gary Sobers' languid brilliance at every aspect of the game and the fearsome pace of Hall and Griffith. Through my schoolboy's eyes, the series seemed to be played in good humour although I doubt if Colin Cowdrey was laughing much when his arm was broken at Lords. I had always thought Griffith was bowling but Wisden says it was Hall so it must have been.

England's team was pretty memorable too. Apart from Cowdrey, it included Dexter and Barrington, Trueman and Statham but it was the West Indians that really caught my imagination. Although, years later, I would come to cherish and admire players such as Botham and Gower, my first cricketing heroes were Sobers and Kanhai.

The great 20th century philosopher Rod Stewart[1] sang that the first cut is the deepest. In my case, he was absolutely spot on. I still support West Indies against anyone except England and I was delighted when Brian Lara reclaimed his Test record from Matthew Hayden. I was delighted for three reasons; Firstly, Hayden's score was against Zimbabwe so shouldn't really count. Secondly, Matthew Hayden is Australian and thirdly because Matthew Hayden is Matthew Hayden.

Hutton (364) had held the world Test record for 19 years, Sobers (365 not out) held it for 36 years and Lara (375) for 9 years. Having bludgeoned Zimbabwe into submission - 'Made it, Ma! Top of the world!' - Hayden's 380 was overtaken within 26 weeks. Oh joy!

If you are sitting in the pub and there is a lull in the conversation, a good question to ask is who played Test cricket for England in the 1940s, 50s, 60s and 70s? Wives and girlfriends will look to the ceiling and start talking about whatever wives and girlfriends talk about. Americans will look bemused and leave the pub and you can get down to the serious business of talking about cricket. So a pretty good result all round. In the interest of political correctness and a quiet life, I would like to point out that I do realise that some wives and girlfriends are interested in cricket. This is a good thing and they of course would be very welcome to join in the discussion.

The answer is Brian Close. He was picked for England at the tender age of 18 years and 149 days in 1949. He had an outstanding first season, including playing in the Gentlemen

---

1   I am indebted to Rob McKeith for pointing out that the song was actually written by Ysuf Islam, surely a leg spinner in his younger days.

versus Players match. Close did well for the Players and top-scored with 65. When he reached his fifty, the Gentlemen's wicket keeper, Billy Griffith congratulated Close by saying, 'Well played, Brian', with Close replying, 'Thank you, Billy'. However, Close had not referred to Griffith as 'Mister', and ten days later was called to see Brian Sellers, a former captain and member of the Yorkshire committee, who reprimanded Close for his effrontery. Ah, those were the days. When everyone knew their place and if you didn't, some prat like Brian Sellers was there to remind you.

Close was a member of the England side that played the West Indies in 1963. He played some typically heroic innings, particularly at Lords after Cowdrey's arm was broken. He batted nearly 4 hours for 70 and took countless blows on the body. Helmets, of course, had not been invented and there was no restriction on the number of bouncers. When he only had the tail to bat with, he started to walk down the pitch to Hall and Griffith, which is rather like being in the outside lane of the M6 trying to swat the cars as they come towards you.

Close was from Yorkshire at a time when men were men and Come Dancing was something the missus watched on Saturday night while you were having a beer after the match. He was a talented all round sportsman. A right-handed golfer with a single figure handicap, he changed to left handed and within a month his handicap was in single figures again! (Gary Sobers did the same. It just isn't fair is it?). Brian Close also played football for Arsenal and there surely must be a role for him at the club today. Some of the poor dears seem to fall over and get hurt so easily these days. Perhaps Close could show them how to look after themselves?

Close's Arsenal career ended one year when Yorkshire's opening match of the season against the MCC at Lords clashed with Arsenal's Cup match. Close tried to play in both games but, due to a misunderstanding, arrived at Highbury half an hour late. You would think they could have delayed the match wouldn't you? The end of April is, after all, the cricket season. Arsenal lost 3-1 and Close was sacked.

Others have tried to combine the two games. Arthur Milton, also an Arsenal player, was the last person to represent England at both football and cricket. He got one cap for England, a 2-2 draw against Austria in 1951. He retired from football in 1955 to concentrate on his cricket for Gloucestershire. In 1958 he scored a debut century for England against New Zealand. He opened the batting with M.J.K Smith - also a double international (cricket and rugby). The modern equivalent would be say Phil Neville opening with Jonny Wilkinson. Seems unlikely to happen, although Phil did play in the same Lancashire county youth team as Freddie Flintoff and was considered by many a better player.

It has become increasingly difficult to combine the two sports and is now virtually impossible since the football season ends well into the cricket season and then starts again a few weeks later.

Chris Balderstone played cricket for Yorkshire, England and Leicestershire. I am told by my friend Steve, born in Leeds, that this is the correct order to put them in. Balderstone was also a professional footballer, playing for Huddersfield Town, Carlisle and Doncaster Rovers. To him goes the distinction of being the last person to play first class cricket and league football on the same day. Furthermore, he did it in real style.

Towards the end of the 1975 cricket season, Leicestershire secured enough bonus points during their game against Derbyshire at Chesterfield to win the County Championship. Chris Balderstone was 51 not out at the end of the second day. He changed into his football kit and rushed to Doncaster to play in an evening league match against Brentford. Luckily, metatarsals hadn't been discovered back then, so injury worries were less of a concern. Next day he completed his century in the morning and then took 3 wickets to help beat Derbyshire. True class!

Chris Balderstone played 2 Tests against the 1976 West Indians. The star of that team was Viv Richards who also played football for Antigua in a World Cup qualifying match. Richards was once bowled by Steve Ogrizovic, the Coventry goalkeeper who was playing for the Minor Counties against the touring West Indians. Ogrizovic played football against Phil Neale, probably the last true professional cricket and football player. Neale played league football with Ian Botham at Scunthorpe and was thus able to secure his services for Worcestershire when Botham fell out with Somerset. Which brings us back to Brian Close who was Botham's first captain at Somerset. Life is full of coincidences isn't it?

Brian Close once caught Gary Sobers hooking. Nothing special in that you might think except that Close was fielding at short leg at the time. He never moved an inch and caught the ball when it got the under edge of Sobers' bat. When asked what would have happened if the ball had hit him on the head, he replied that the catch would have been taken at gully. True Yorkshire grit!

Close had a part in the great soap opera of the time that was Yorkshire County Cricket Club. It also starred Fred Trueman (later to be related to Raquel Welch by marriage but, alas for him, not his own), Ray Illingworth (famous for winning the Ashes Down Under in 1971 and 'relieving himself at the Pavilion end') and Geoff Boycott (famous for being Geoff Boycott).

If you were being generous you would say that Geoffrey Boycott was a single minded professional who held the batting together for England and Yorkshire on many occasions. The alternative view is that he was a selfish sod who was more interested in his own batting average than the success of the team. This is the man that was dropped by England in 1967 for scoring too slowly, after making 246 not out, even though England won the match. It took him nine and a half hours against a mediocre Indian attack that had lost two of its main bowlers. He never really lost this obsessive approach to batting. In 1982, playing against Warwickshire, he was involved in a record 10th wicket partnership with Graham Stevenson. They scored 149 of which Stevenson, Yorkshire's No.11, scored 115.

There were many other highlights of course. 151 first class centuries. A match winning 146 for Yorkshire in the 1965 Gillette Cup Final (so he could attack bowling if he felt like it). A hundred on his return to Test cricket against Australia at Trent Bridge in 1977 but, being Boycott, he had to run out the local hero Derek Randall in the process. His hundredth first class century came later in the series, fittingly at Headingley, when he on-drove Greg Chappell to the boundary. He averaged 100 in an English first class season twice - the only player ever to do it until Mark Ramprakash did it for the second successive season in 2007.

The possibly apocryphal story goes that Boycott reckoned he had finally worked out how to play Johnny Gleeson, the Australian 'leggie' who tormented England in 1971. He was surprised when his batting partner, Basil D'Oliveira, excitedly informed him that he felt he too had found a way to combat the spinner. Boycott murmured as they headed for the pavilion: 'Aye, that's fine - but don't tell the others.'

Yorkshire got a lot of bad press when Boycott was captain, with the implication that there wasn't enough team spirit. This simply wasn't true. Apparently, before each match, the players each put 50p in a kitty and anyone that ran Boycott out won the pot. This helped create a really good team spirit, it just didn't necessarily include the captain (by the way, there was a 'rollover' most weeks).

A favourite Boycott witticism, when asked how to play a particularly difficult bowler, is 'from t'other end'. Well, in 1976 he had carried this to its logical conclusion and wasn't at either end. He had judiciously made himself unavailable for England against the fearsome West Indian pace attack. This led to the possibly unique situation at one point in the series when the average age of England's first three batsmen - Close (45), Edrich (39) and Steele (35) was greater than their combined Test batting average. Boycott wasn't available to play for England for about three years. Seemingly he didn't think a Scotsman (poor old Mike Denness) should captain England. You can see his point but unfortunately his preferred alternative was himself.

Back in 1976, I was convinced that our team spirit, not to mention the bowling attack, would be helped by the addition of a 6' 6" West Indian but where to find one? Michael Holding hadn't signed up for a county as far as I knew, so he might be available. Hampshire would probably have a prior claim on Andy Roberts but it might be worth a try.

Help came from an unlikely source. Nick, the squash player, had proved to be just that at the Clifton Hampden match - a squash player. However, when discussing his availability for the return match he mentioned that he worked with a West Indian called Vernon who played cricket. Should he try and get him to play? Is the Pope a Catholic? Does Didier Drogba dive? Does Kevin Pietersen have a mirror in his bedroom? Yes, of course! It would mean that Nick secured his place in the side but there's a price to pay for everything.

The two 'friends of friends' at the first match had indeed turned up and proved to be enthusiastic but not particularly good at cricket (this is of course all relative). One had scored 0 and the other 2. The 2 should have been given as leg byes but it's in the book and it made him joint 4th top scorer on the day. I felt no real obligation to ask them to play again the following year, although if one of them had scored 50 we might have become best friends.

The other nine players all wanted to have another go so, with Vernon taking one of the spare places, I only had to find one more player, preferably someone who could actually play cricket. Ray had a friend, Mike, who played cricket and also came from Yorkshire - the two don't always go together, and he agreed to play. This was 1977 and he is still turning out at the Clifton Hampden match today.

The day of the match dawned and we all met at the Plough on Sunday morning. Nick turned up with Vernon. I think I hid my disappointment at noticing that he was only about 5' 9" but on the credit side he did have his own kit. However, as he downed his third pint, I was getting a little concerned. Everyone approaches big matches in different ways. Personally, I only drink lime juice and water before a match. I do this partly because of the inevitable excesses of the night before but also to try and set a good example to the rest of the team. This never works and I fully recognise the rest of the team's inalienable human right to drink as many pints as they want to before the match.

Our game was due to start at 2.30. At about 2.0 o'clock I suggested some fielding practice before the game started. This was met with a mixture of laughter, scorn and mocking sympathy. A captain's burden is truly a heavy one.

We eventually started the game at about ten to three. I won the toss, studied the pitch very carefully and, not wanting the game to be over by 3.30, put Clifton Hampden in to bat. The opposition had a similar line up to the previous year. Sadly, so did we.

Actually we got off to great start. Hugh took early wickets and Vernon, coming on as first change, bowled pretty quickly, considering he was only 5' 9". He took three wickets and Clifton Hampden were reeling at 97 for 7. Unfortunately, Vernon began to fade, I knew that fifth pint had been a mistake, and Clifton Hampden's lower order began to give him some stick. Eventually, they were all out for 167. We took tea in a sombre mood. My own two overs, coming on to tighten things up during the lower order mayhem, had cost 17 runs. We had let them off the hook and now we had to bat rather well to win, or even save, the match. The problem was that the last time most of the side had batted was in the Clifton Hampden game the previous year and we all knew what happened then.

Rather than hold him back, and because I noticed that the club bar had opened, I decided to unleash Vernon straight away. He opened with Ray and scored a very elegant and promising single down to fine leg before perishing in the following over, trying to hit the opening bowler into the next county. The ace up my sleeve, my 'ringer', my West Indian superstar was out for 1. When I had said to him play your natural game, I didn't mean it literally. What I really meant was, play yourself in, score at least 50 then play your natural game.

1 for 1 was not the start I had hoped for. Next in was Ray's friend, Mike from Yorkshire. It was his first time at Clifton Hampden and it was almost his last. He batted well for a while and then was adjudged LBW. To say he wasn't happy with the decision doesn't really do him justice. I made the mistake of trying to sympathise with him in the changing room and learnt that he hadn't driven 50 f***ing miles to be given out LB f***ing W half way down the f***ing pitch.

I knew exactly how he felt and couldn't have put it more eloquently myself when, 20 minutes later, I was given out in almost identical circumstances. I became one of five LBW decisions in our innings (I try to explain this phenomenon in Chapter 6).

Next man in was Clive. An inconvenient family wedding had deprived us of Roger and so Clive played in his place. He was a philosophy lecturer, darts player, jazz drummer, footballer, carp fisherman but regrettably not a cricketer. At least he had turned up, which wasn't always the case in future years, and he seemed very keen to make his debut. When I say debut, I don't just mean Clifton Hampden debut. He revealed to me as he was going out to bat that this was his first ever 'proper' game of cricket. He was out for 0, LBW naturally.

Without going into all the gruesome details, we were all out for 59, a distinct improvement on 32 but still pretty poor, and over 100 runs short of the opposition's total. We had lasted longer this time so there was no need for the humiliation of a 'beer match'. The Clifton Hampden team seemed quite happy with things, and why shouldn't they? We had our team photo, downed a few beers and agreed to do it all again the following year.

At least at the next game it was unlikely that Rob would be playing under such a handicap, as he had to endure that year. An Irish girl, who had been on friendly terms with a number of the team, sequentially not simultaneously as far as we all knew, had been with us during our pre-match preparations on Saturday. She had got rather tired and emotional - more in the literal sense rather than the Private Eye one - and in the early hours of Sunday morning demanded that someone take her to Didcot railway station. Rob had been lying in his tent on his back, oblivious to the world, when the crazy colleen brought the canvas, wet with the early morning dew, crashing down on him, with her on top. We think she was upset because he had been ignoring her. This scene took place in the tented city that was my parents' garden. They were blissfully unaware of the emotional and physical trauma being inflicted on various members of the team. Eventually she was taken to Didcot but Rob's carefully honed plans to be in peak physical and mental condition for the match were in ruins. I'm sure that Steve Harmison doesn't have to put up with this sort of thing; or perhaps he does?

4. Don't Think Twice, It's All Right

1978. David Ivon Gower pulled his first ball in Test cricket for four and Ian Terrance Botham became the first player ever to score a century and take 8 wickets in an innings, in the same Test match. On a more prosaic level, we had to try and avoid a third successive defeat at the hands of Clifton Hampden's occasional Sunday team.

Being a QPR supporter, I was accustomed to disappointment in sport but that didn't mean I enjoyed it. You have to be a Scottish football supporter for that. The 1975/76 season had been QPR's greatest season, and in a way the most disappointing. I can name the team that season a lot quicker than I can name the current QPR team. Parkes, Clement and Gillard, Webb and McClintock, Hollins, Masson and Francis, Thomas, Givens and Bowles. Some may think it is sad to be able to name the QPR team of 30 years ago; I say it shows loyalty, commitment and a good memory.

What a team! Phil Parkes - better than Shilton at clean sheets and balance sheets. Dave Clement and Ian Gillard, both marvellous fullbacks in defence and attack. Dave Webb and Frank McClintock - solid as a rock. OK, they used to play for Chelsea and Arsenal but they were forgiven for that. John Hollins, another ex-Chelsea man and a gritty midfield competitor. Don Masson came from a time when Scotland used to produce skilful footballers. Gerry Francis, England's youngest captain at 24, an outstanding attacking midfielder whose career was cut short by injury. Don Givens, born in Limerick, was Ireland's centre forward, and Dave Thomas a mazy winger from Burnley.

Finally, the jewel in the crown, Stan Bowles. As a young player, he had fallen out with Malcolm Allison at Manchester City and had arrived at QPR via Bury, Crewe and Carlisle. Rodney Marsh had just been sold to Man City when Stan arrived and took on the No.10 shirt as his own. He was an artist and he didn't look back. He only played for England 5 times, under three different managers, despite being one of the most skilful players of his generation. If he'd been able to pass a betting shop like he could pass a football........

April 1976 and three games to go, two of which were at home and if all were won then nothing could stop the league title coming to Loftus Road. Disastrously lost 3-2 away to Norwich but then, two days later beat Arsenal 2-1. Final game of the season beat Leeds 2-0 at home (I was there with Steve, a Leeds supporter for his sins!). Could still do it if Liverpool failed to beat Wolves. To show how things have changed in football, Liverpool's final game was on the 4th May, 10 days after QPR had played their last match. So Liverpool knew exactly what they had to do to win the league. Also, the game wasn't on TV so I had to listen to it on the radio. Wolves scored first to give some hope and agonisingly, held the lead till the 77th minute. Then Liverpool scored three times to win 3-1. Bastards! Liverpool were always winning the league, surely they wouldn't have minded missing out just this once. 1976 was QPR's one and only chance, they will never have another opportunity.

Until recently, although the big teams have always dominated the league, at least unfancied teams did win sometimes. Incredible as it seems now, Derby (1975), Nottingham Forest (1978), Aston Villa (1981), Everton (1987) Leeds (1992) and Blackburn (1995), have all won the top league, against the odds, in relatively recent times. 1976 should have been QPR's year! Nowadays, only three or four clubs can possibly win the league. Chelsea would like to think only one can win it. Football is diminished as a result.

Back in 1978, I had my own problems. How to avoid another defeat at the hands of Clifton Hampden. I had rather foolishly introduced a sort of rule that if someone played one year and was available the next year then they would be automatically selected. No elitism for the Mike Harfield XI. No dropping of lifelong friends simply on the grounds that they were useless at cricket. No bloody chance of winning!

My loyalty would have been sorely put to the test if I had been successful with one of my more exotic recruitment plans. Around this time, I worked with, and was good friends with, Mike Gower – cousin of David. Unfortunately, the cricketing gods had seen fit to bequest all the cricket talent on only one side of the family so asking Mike to play would not have helped the team. Despite buying him several expensive lunches, I could never get Mike to invite his cousin to the Clifton Hampden weekend even after David had retired and didn't have the excuse that he was playing in a Test match.

So that year, the team followed a similar pre-match ritual to the one that had served us so badly the two previous years. Saturday lunchtime drinking in Oxford followed by a team meeting in the Plough on Saturday night concluding with a few drinks to settle the stomach and calm the nerves on Sunday lunchtime before the match.

When we eventually all managed to make the long trek from the Plough to the ground, the Clifton Hampden team looked pleased to see us, and why not! Most of them were knocking up on the outfield or 'practising before the match' as it is sometimes known. Many of them had also played the day before, whereas half our team hadn't picked up a cricket bat or ball in anger since the previous year.

The portents were not good and seeing the name Cox-Rogers on their team sheet did not help our confidence. He was an aggressive middle order batsman who had scored heavily against us in the previous games. He had a simple approach to batting; block the straight ones and hit the others to the boundary. Since there were plenty of 'others' when we bowled, he tended to score a lot of runs.

I went out to the square with the Clifton Hampden captain for the traditional tossing of the coin even though by now we both knew that, whatever happened, they would be batting. Sure enough, I won the toss and after looking at the pitch as though I was trying to decide what to do, I invited them to bat.

I've been looking at pitches before, during and after cricket matches for years now and I still haven't really got a clue what I'm looking at or for. I don't think I'm alone though. In the first Test at Brisbane in 2002, Nasser Hussain won the toss and having presumably discussed the matter with other 'pitch experts', invited Australia to bat. They proceeded to score 364 for two by stumps on the first day, Hayden and Ponting both scoring centuries. Admittedly, England's cause was not helped by the horrific injury to Simon Jones but the damage had already been done before he went off. Australia were eventually all out for 492 and went on to win the match by 384 runs. England, batting last, as you tend to do when putting the opposition in, were all out for 79 in their second innings.

Hussain obviously doesn't read his Wisdens. In the First Test at Headingley in 1989, David Gower won the toss and, probably for equally sound reasons, asked Allan Border to have a bat. The Australians scored 601 for seven so I think we can assume that the gamble failed. Mark Taylor and Steve Waugh both got their maiden Test centuries and England lost by 210 runs. It started a run of success for the Australians that lasted sixteen years. If England had batted first, as patently they should have done, who knows how things might have turned out. Actually, it's likely that things would have turned out much the same way. Later in the series, at Nottingham, Australia scored 301 on the first day without losing a wicket but at least they were not put in to bat on that occasion.

Just to show that it is not an exclusively English affliction, Dravid put England in at Mumbai in the Third Test in March 2006. This despite the fact that they were 1-0 up in the three match series and had two world class spinners in the side who presumably would have liked to have a bowl on a turning pitch on the last day. England scored 400 in their first innings and when India batted in their second innings, on the fifth day, they were all out for 100. England won the match by 212 runs. Heath Streak was another who no doubt regretted putting the opposition in, at Perth in 2003. Australia declared at 735 for 6 (Hayden made his 380 in this match) and went on to win by an innings and 175 runs.

Even Australian captains can be lured into the trap. In the Second Test in 2005, Ricky Ponting put England in at Edgbaston. In mitigation, England had been well and truly hammered in the First Test at Lords so perhaps he was feeling a touch over confident. What he failed to take into account was McGrath getting injured just before the match began. You could say that it worked as England were bowled out on the first day in just over 79 overs but not before they had scored 407 runs! England went on to thrash Australia by 2 runs.

No less an authority than W.G Grace said 'When you win the toss - bat. If you are in doubt, think about it, then bat. If you have very big doubts consult a colleague - then bat.' He was of course referring to first class cricket. Village cricket is somewhat different. If you have some good batsmen in the side then you will probably want to bat first. If you have a strong bowling attack and you want to be home early, the captain might put the opposition in. If, like us at the time, you haven't anyone that seriously resembles a decent batsman or bowler then it is safer to invite the other side to bat. The opposition scoring 250 for 3 and you being all out for 15 is marginally less embarrassing than batting first, being all out for 15 and the other side knocking off the runs in a couple of overs.

So it was that in 1978, Clifton Hampden went out to bat. The sun was shining on the cornfield. Spectators were scattered round the ground, not actually watching the cricket but at least they were there. All eleven of our players had turned up. Life was good. Hugh was inspired and took 3 early wickets. We had them in trouble at 35 for 3. Then Cox-Rogers came in. If we could get him then we were surely home and dry. He murdered us, hitting the ball over the pavilion, into the cornfield and to all parts of Oxfordshire. When Vernon finally got him out, they were up to 130.

Learning from the previous year, I had wisely held myself back and waited for Cox-Rogers to be out before coming on to bowl. One of the few advantages of being captain is choosing not to bowl if the opposition's best batsman is smashing the ball all over the place. Ray Illingworth was a past master at this. It worked for me on this occasion. I got a couple of cheap wickets and Clifton Hampden were finally all out for 156.

Once again, we had let them off the hook and it was a quieter than usual bunch of players that contemplated the huge tea that Clifton Hampden had provided for us as usual. The reason for the subdued air was this. Even though most of the team had drunk too much the night before, preferred to be in the Plough on Sunday lunchtime rather than practise and hadn't played since the previous year, everyone still wanted to win. Not 'win at all costs' or 'we can't enjoy it if we don't win', just a natural competitive aspiration to do ourselves justice, and try to win.

We went out to bat and flattered to deceive. A good shot here, a boundary there but wickets fell at an alarmingly fast rate. At one point, Vernon looked like justifying the Gary Sobers billing that I had given him but he perished after a quickfire 20. Some late order forehand smashes from Nick the squash player helped get us to a final total of 84. Although we had done a bit better, there was no hiding the fact that we had lost comprehensively once again.

The sun went down and so did the beer. Owen, one of the stalwarts of Clifton Hampden CC, did a barbecue for us all and the pain of defeat diminished a little. Girlfriends asked how we had got on and seemed happy with the response that we had come second.

Looking on the bright side, we had improved on the previous two years. 32, 59, 84...........at this rate, assuming the Clifton Hampden total stayed about the same, we should catch up with them some time in the mid 1980s.

5. Fourth Time Around

Can it really be just a coincidence that 1979 was the year that 'Apocalypse Now' came out and Margaret Thatcher won her first general election? 'Where there is discord, may we bring harmony. Where there is error, may we bring truth. Where there is doubt, may we bring faith. And where there is despair, may we bring hope'. What a load of old bollocks but somehow it aptly summed up my own problems at the time.

We had lost to Clifton Hampden three years in a row. Two of the team had decided to get married the previous year (not to each other, although I would like to point out that we are an 'inclusive' team and had they married each other, they would have still been welcome in the dressing room). On top of that, my West Indian ringer enjoyed himself rather too much before the match for my liking. Troubled times indeed.

On the positive side, a few of the team had actually started to play cricket at other times apart from the annual Clifton Hampden game. Being generally optimistic by nature, I took this as an encouraging sign. One of these was Colin, who had been sipping his Fullers ESB very slowly at the original meeting, when we first came up with the idea of the Clifton Hampden cricket match. I had been at Abingdon School with Colin and had witnessed his greatest hour on the cricket field (actually it was almost two hours). It was in a game for our Junior Colts XI against Radley College. Radley was a much posher school than ours (Lord Ted Dexter had gone there for goodness sake!) and Colin, who even then saw everything in terms of the class struggle, was in his element.

Radley batted first and scored 155 for 8 declared, a lot of runs at our age level and more than enough for us. When we went out after tea, Colin opened and batted for nearly two hours. He simply blocked every ball and made no attempt to get any runs. He was determined not to give his wicket away to those 'posh bastards' as he so quaintly described the opposition. Wickets fell regularly at the other end but Colin remained resolutely at the crease. At the close we were 47 for 9, Colin was 6 not out and we had achieved a draw. The Radley players were extremely pissed off. Colin was in Seventh Heaven. Geoffrey Boycott and Karl Marx eat your hearts out.

If you are wondering how I can recall the scores in such detail forty years after the event, the answer is the school magazine, which obviously I kept so that I could help Colin work out his career batting average should he want to do it. Colin is mentioned that year as having 'distinguished himself as a stone-walling match saver'. Qualities that had been noticeable by their absence from him or anyone else at the Clifton Hampden matches so far. However, now Colin had started playing again, there was light at the end of the corridor of uncertainty.

We all met up as usual in Oxford on the Saturday. The talk was of cricket and of Maggie Thatcher whom the electorate had just asked to run the country. She had got rid of free milk for school children, what could she do now that she was in charge of the whole shop? It didn't take long to find out. She enjoyed the nickname 'Iron Lady' but was probably less keen on 'Attila The Hen', thought to have been first coined by Sir Ian Gilmour. She was good at facing down the miners and giving the European Commission a good handbagging but she really didn't have a sense of humour. She once said about her deputy, William Whitelaw ' Every Prime Minister needs a Willy.' She just could not understand why everyone around her fell about in hysterics.

Politics just got us agitated and was not good for the team's equilibrium. It was safer to stick to cricket. The West Indies had just retained the one-day World Cup against England in the final at Lords. Viv Richards scored an unbeaten century and the West Indies reached 286 for 9. Even though it was a 60 overs competition in those days, this was considered a pretty good score. Brearley and Boycott opened in England's reply. Wisden reports that 'Boycott occupied 17 overs to reach double figures.' It can't be much fun facing Roberts, Holding, Croft and Garner but what did he think he was doing? Playing for a draw? Playing for his average? Having a net?

To be fair to Boycott, which is not always an easy thing

to do, Brearley was not much quicker at the other end. It's even more bizarre when you look at the batting still to come for England. Derek Randall, Graham Gooch, David Gower, Ian Botham and Wayne Larkins! Brearley may have a brain the size of Suffolk but it seems that it wasn't in use that day. A little imagination with the batting order might have been a good idea for a start. Clearly, Botham should have opened with Boycott with instructions to run him out if he didn't get a move on. This had worked in a Test match in New Zealand the year before, when Botham had deliberately run Boycott out because he was batting too slowly and in danger of costing England the match.

Inevitably it all ended in tears with England needing 158 from the last 22 overs. 7 wickets went down for 11 runs, as Joel Garner and Colin Croft wiped out the middle and lower order. England were all out for 194.

We could hopefully learn from this for our game at Clifton Hampden. Someone batting 17 overs for 10 runs would be just fine. Looking round the team in the Plough on Saturday night this didn't seem a very likely prospect. Rob was always good for double figures, pints not runs unfortunately. Steve seemed to have hollow legs given the amount he was knocking back. Clive looked very relaxed considering he had not worked out where he was sleeping that night, or perhaps he had. Colin exuded more confidence than you would expect from someone who averaged a little over 4 with the bat in the Clifton Hampden matches.

We woke to a glorious Oxfordshire Sunday morning. Perhaps this would be the day when we would show Clifton Hampden that we weren't just a bunch of amiable poseurs. We got to the ground and said our hellos to the opposition. A lot of familiar faces but I couldn't see Cox-Rogers. Maybe sticking those pins in a wax model had worked?

Clifton Hampden won the toss and batted. This time it was Rob who was on fire. Perhaps it was his hangover that drove him on. Perhaps it was sheer relief at no longer sharing a one-man tent with Steve. Whatever it was, he took 3 quick wickets and Clifton Hampden were staggering at 9 for 3. Rob was a hooker from Sunderland. There are two types of hooker in Sunderland and apparently they are difficult to distinguish from a distance. Rob was the kind you usually find on a rugby pitch. He had a round-shouldered bowling action that eventually became a bit like Jeff Thomson on mogodons. As the years have gone on, the ball has drifted further and further down the leg side. The square leg umpire kept moving back until eventually he was standing in the cornfield and asking for danger money. However, at his peak, Rob was a fearsome sight and that day he was unplayable.

Clifton Hampden started to rebuild their innings but Vernon struck twice and they were really struggling at 40 for 5. With no Cox-Rogers to come in, I thought it was safe to bowl myself. I got an early wicket and the next man came out to bat. He looked about 80 but was probably nearer 70. He had obviously heard about us and had decided to come out of retirement for one last frolic in the sun. I bowled a good length ball, he played and missed by some distance.

Despite having been thrashed in the last three matches, I felt compelled to try and give this guy a chance. I decided to bowl my 'slower ball'. I bowl a sort of military medium but you need to think the Swiss Army rather than say the heroic American 'shock and awe' attack on Baghdad. My slower ball, and we are talking fine degrees of relativity here, is not something I bowled often on the grounds that it was usually thumped over my head for four. On this occasion, my slower ball turned out to be a slow beamer (or full toss if you are being generous). The batsman, who probably had his grand children, if not great-grand children, all watching on the boundary, missed it completely and the ball crashed into his stumps.

His comeback match after 40 odd years in retirement had lasted 2 balls. I felt a little embarrassed but a wicket is a wicket and I had the rather attractive bowling figures of 2 for 2. Needless to say, none of my fellow teammates believed that I had tried to bowl a slower ball, on the basis that to the naked eye it didn't look any slower than my usual efforts. They just assumed that I had spotted a septuagenarian at the other end and had deliberately bowled a beamer at him.

Meanwhile Vernon was cleaning up at the other end and he finished with 5 wickets, or a Michelle Pfeiffer as the Australians call it ('Warney got a Michelle at Old Trafford' is open to all sorts of possible interpretations but it usually means he got 5 wickets in the innings). Incredibly, Clifton Hampden were all out for 56. Surely this was our day? Surely Devon Loch must win the National. Surely Smith must score and Brighton win the Cup? Surely South Africa could score 1 run from 4 balls against Australia?

Clifton Hampden's batting collapse, or as I preferred to see it, our superbly captained bowling and fielding performance, had taken the tea ladies by surprise so we had to go out and bat for 20 minutes before tea. Although we had not experienced it before ourselves, we had all watched enough Test cricket to know that this was a tricky time to bat. We just needed to get through to tea without losing a wicket. Obviously we didn't but thankfully only one went down so at 12 for 1, we ate our tea in confident mood.

After tea, Roger and Vernon were batting together and, in their contrasting ways, looked in control. Roger circumspect and resolute. Vernon commanding and stylish. They had reached 41 with the Promised Land in sight when Vernon, possibly noticing that the club bar had opened, tried to launch the ball into space. He missed and was clean bowled. Never mind, it gave someone else the chance to have a bat before our inevitable victory.

Ray went in and was bowled immediately, 41-3. This brought the captain, trying to look calm, to the crease. As I joined Roger in the middle I thought I detected a look of trapped panic in his face, rather like Richard Nixon at a hostile press conference. However, as he often looked like this, I chose to ignore it. Whatever encouraging and supportive words I said to him clearly didn't work. The next over, Roger, hitherto the epitome of patience, was caught behind cutting, 42-4. Then came Nick, the squash player, batting worryingly high at number six. A forehand smash for two and a drop shot into the bowler's hands, 44-5.

Next man in was Colin, the erstwhile 'stone-walling match saver'. We had been friends since school and together we had got the Clifton Hampden event off the ground from its inception. What could be more appropriate than the two of us knocking off the remaining few runs to record our first win?

Colin played back to his third ball. The ball hit his pad, the appeal went up and he was adjudged LBW, 44-6. Oh my God! No, this can't be happening. Replacing Colin was Clive playing in his second match........ever. Clifton Hampden normally used eight or nine bowlers against us. This time the opening bowlers were still on and showing no signs of coming off. The jovial bonhomie and chat of previous years was noticeable by its absence. This time it was serious!

Clive came down the wicket to his first ball and played an immaculate forward defensive shot. Unfortunately he missed the ball by about a foot. The wicket keeper was so surprised that he also missed it, which was just as well as Clive was about three feet out of his crease. By this time, my nerves were so shot to pieces that I failed to call for a bye which would have given us a much needed extra run closer to the total. At the end of the over, I went to have a chat with Clive. I couldn't really say 'play your natural game' because I had no idea what his 'natural game' was or whether he even had one.

Instead I relied on the other good old faithful 'don't do anything silly'. I'm sure this was very helpful advice because the next ball he faced, Clive came down the wicket and played exactly the same impeccable forward defensive shot. Clive aimed his bat in the general direction of extra cover and seemed perplexed not to see the ball going there. Instead he got an inside edge, the ball went down to fine leg and we ran a single.

Somehow Clive and I kept out the Clifton Hampden bowlers and we managed to scrape together the remaining 12 runs that we needed. We had won by 4 wickets! The feeling of relief was palpable. Winning isn't everything but, all other things being equal, it certainly beats losing. We had started the game more in hope than expectation but now the embarrassments of the earlier matches were a distant memory. Clifton Hampden were generous in their congratulations and we celebrated well into the night.

The following year buoyed by our victory and secure in the knowledge that half the team was now playing regular cricket, I had the confidence to bat first when I won the toss. We were rewarded with a total of 167 all out. Colin finally made some runs and Hugh hit a sparkling cameo including three sixes. The personnel were very much the same as the first game but in the space of four years we were now actually looking like a real cricket team.

We bowled out Clifton Hampden for 130 and we had won our second match in a row. What's more, we had done it without Vernon. For some reason, probably not unconnected to the lift Rob had given him back to London after the game the previous year, he wasn't available to play. The usual way back to London from Clifton Hampden was along the M40 but it didn't generally include visiting High Wycombe and certainly not more than once. Like Clint Eastwood asking the taxi driver in Coogan's Bluff 'How many stores called Bloomingdale's are in this town?', Vernon was heard to enquire how many towns there were called High Wycombe. Together with Rob's generous use of the hard shoulder, the unscheduled visits to High Wycombe were enough to make Vernon turn pale and it took him some time to recover.

Vernon's replacement that year was Bob, an old school

friend of Steve. Bob had no pretensions to be a cricketer. He had a somewhat unconventional method of stopping balls that were hit in his direction when fielding. He would stop everything with his shins, only using his hands to pick the ball up and throw it to the fielder nearest him. We assumed that Bob was wearing shin pads, but later it turned out that he wasn't. He just thought that was the way you stopped a cricket ball. He was also the answer to every village captain's hardest cricketing decision. Who to bat at No.11?

Bob played a few games for us in the '80s and '90s, ending up with a batting average of 0.5. One year, he flew in from South Africa accompanied by a newly acquired girlfriend. It soon became apparent that Ingrid was a much better cricketer than Bob. How to get her into the team? Would Bob feel his manhood under threat or would he just be grateful? Could Ingrid put up with the inevitable 'bowl a maiden over' jokes? Would players be longer in the showers after the game? In the end, Bob retained his place in the team but it was a close run thing.

England cricket captains have it easy really. The batting order is predetermined; indeed the England batting order is so inflexible that it sometimes seems that players have their batting position written into their contracts. The England captain doesn't have to make sure that someone is doing the teas, doesn't have to ensure that the hot water is on for the showers, doesn't have to contend with the wife of his opening bowler coming onto the pitch and hauling him off to deal with some problem at home. By and large, captaining England must be a piece of cake and when Gatting had the job, a very large one at that.

6. Blind Willie McTell

Umpiring in village cricket is not, on the face of it, that difficult. If you can count to six and are familiar with the basic umpiring signals, you should be able to cope.

There are no instant action replays to show that you were in fact asleep for the stumping appeal that you gave not out when the batsman was three feet out of his crease. Wides are pretty straightforward - you don't give them unless the ball knocks out the cover point or square leg fielder. Was it a run, a bye or a leg bye - does it really matter? Well actually, yes it does. If you are out the next ball for 0, for your third duck in a row, you would definitely want that leg bye down as a run.

But this is all small beer compared to the issue that has ended lifelong friendships, caused dressing rooms to be rearranged, made normally mild mannered men, who love their wives, fill out their tax forms and are kind to animals, go apoplectic. Yes, please give a warm welcome to the LBW law.

In very basic terms, LBW means you can be out if the ball hits your pad and was going on to hit the stumps. Some people who umpire never get beyond this simple interpretation of the rules. There is, of course, a labyrinth of interpretations that lie behind the LBW law. The ball has to hit the pad in line with the stumps to be out. If the ball pitches outside the leg stump you can't be out. Would the ball have gone over the stumps or down the leg side? Before you do your next stint of umpiring, ask any club cricketer to bowl six balls at an exposed set of stumps and see how many times he hits. It won't be very many.

It's unusual in 'friendly' village matches to have official umpires so the players, who have already batted or are due to bat later, usually carry out the role. I think it's fair to say that it is not the most popular of jobs. It is amazing how many players need to go to the toilet or check on the children or hide behind a tree when the captain is trying to find some volunteers to do the umpiring.

The game can't start without umpires so eventually two players will be press-ganged or blackmailed into doing it. You might think that doing the umpiring when your own side is batting would give the batting side a distinct advantage. In our case, the exact opposite was the case. In the first five years of the Clifton Hampden match, we had 14 LBW appeals upheld against us, all given by members of our own team. That is an average of 2.8 per game, curiously enough, very close to my own batting average during the same period.

In our first game there were 3 LBW decisions against us and in the second game, 5 LBWs! These in games when we were all out for 32 and 59 respectively. As I was a victim both times, I feel I can speak authoritatively on the subject.

Why would players give so many members of their own team out LBW? It could be malice or it could be stupidity. I would like to think it isn't simply malice; well, not every time anyway. There's no doubt that it can be very amusing to hear a team-mate seething after an LBW decision and listening to his explanation that the ball pitched so far outside the leg stump it should have been given as a wide. But maliciousness can not explain all LBW decisions.

No, in most cases I think it is just plain stupidity. It's true, if you are not used to umpiring, that often your first instinctive reaction when the ball hits the pad and there's a loud appeal, is to twitch the right index finger. In our early matches, whenever the ball hit the pads, there was frequently a response that Pavlov's dogs would have been proud of.

It doesn't matter how often you explain to some people that if the ball pitches outside the leg stump you can't be out LBW and if the ball hits the pad outside the line of the stumps you can't be out LBW and if your side is 24 for 5 you can't be out LBW. Some umpires will always give the Pavlovian response and the batsman has to walk. These individuals need to be identified very early on and not allowed near a white coat under any circumstances. Unfortunately, it took me about five years to work this out.

When we were batting in the first Clifton Hampden match, the wickets were falling so quickly that with two players batting, two players umpiring, two players padding up, one scoring and one beating up the guy who had just given him out LBW, I almost felt like calling a group of consultants to advise me what to do next.

During the first five years of our games, Clifton Hampden had 3 LBW decisions against them compared to our 14. I hasten to add that this doesn't mean the Clifton Hampden players were cheating, they were simply utilising the unwritten section of the LBW law - 'give the benefit of doubt to the batsman' or put another way 'use your bloody common sense!'

The pub team I play for these days - the Ash Tree CC - has got round the problem. You can't be out LBW. Whatever you do, even if it's on the back foot plumb in front of middle stump, you can't be out. You might think this would lead to a glorified form of French cricket but apart from encouraging you to play across the line rather more than perhaps you should, it seems to work. If only I had thought to suggest that to the Clifton Hampden captain all those years ago.

One of my recruits in the '80s was Duncan. Good bloke, good tennis player, good footballer, rubbish umpire. It happened that he was umpiring in one of the games during our unbeaten run of matches. We were only chasing 117 and Roger had opened the batting. By his own admission, Roger is not one of the world's most graceful batsmen. Think Chris Tavare rather than David Gower. Nevertheless, he was usually able to occupy the crease, a basic skill that was noticeably lacking in most members of the team.

He had progressed to 49 not out and we only needed 10 to win. No one had scored a 50 for us, ever, and Roger hadn't scored a 50 since his school days. He was batting within himself, he was focused, he was in the zone; it was just a question of time. Unfortunately, Roger made a fatal error; he let the ball hit his pads. The appeal went up and so did Duncan's finger. I have no idea whether he was really out or not but afterwards Duncan did say that he thought Roger had been in a long time (true), his batting was rather boring (true) and anyway the ball would probably have hit the stumps.

Roger took it well and swore never to speak to the stupid Scottish sod again. I had mixed feelings. Roger's dismissal allowed me to go in and have a bat. As an extra bonus, my 6 not out significantly improved my batting average.

Duncan, who was living in London at the time, has moved back to the safety of Scotland. Whenever the subject of that LBW decision is brought up, which is every year, Roger claims to have moved on and it doesn't bother him any more but has Hilary Clinton forgiven Monica Lewinsky? Has Michael Howard forgiven Ann Widdecombe? Has Alex Ferguson ever forgiven anyone? I rest my case.

Many years later, Duncan made one of his occasional forays south to play in the Clifton Hampden match. We batted first and Roger opened the innings. It is difficult to say who was the most horrified when Roger looked up and asked for a guard, only to find Duncan occupying the umpire's position. When Duncan had volunteered to start the umpiring, I had forgotten that Roger was opening the batting. No really, I had.

A clearly shaken Duncan then glanced to his right to see the identity of Roger's opening partner. It was Roger's son. Although only a toddler when the original LBW incident had occurred, Richard was very familiar with the story. Indeed, it had been told to him so many times that he probably knew the details better than many people who had actually been involved.

Now his father's antagonist confronted him in the flesh. Would history repeat itself? Would the family curse fall upon the son? Would GBH be committed if LBW was given? Muttering obscure literary references from 'Macbeth' and looking decidedly agitated, Roger asked Duncan for 'middle and leg'. What followed lay to rest a quarter of a century of Anglo Scottish enmity. LBW appeals were turned down, snicks behind were ignored, 'no balls' were liberally granted, and that was just in the first over.

One no ball in Roger's innings was so late that he was already back in the pavilion taking off his pads when Duncan called it. On and on Roger and son batted for an apparent eternity before Duncan was relieved of his post, his duty done, the curse lifted and lifelong grudges put aside.

Duncan and Roger chatted like bosom pals at teatime and Roger was the first to go to his aid when Duncan, forgetting he was no longer twenty three, badly damaged his rotator cuff in an ill advised dive at cover point. The game finished late and we retired to the club bar. Whether he was drinking to mask the anguish of another defeat at Clifton Hampden or the pain in his shoulder or simply celebrating the settlement of the LBW debt wasn't clear, but Duncan was in his cups after the match.

So much so that he completely forgot that his wife had come with him for the weekend. Katherine, rather surprisingly, had got bored with the cricket and gone back to their tent to read. While Duncan was drinking himself into oblivion, heavy rain had flooded the campsite and Katherine had to be rescued late at night by Steve who was also camping there. Sometime after midnight, a bedraggled Duncan and Katherine arrived at my mother's house, seeking shelter. Their tent had been washed away and they needed somewhere to sleep. How Kath loves these Clifton Hampden weekends.

I settled them down as best I could and stumbled to my own bed. In the morning, my mother rose early to find Duncan, naked except for a tartan jockstrap, sprawled on the sitting room floor nursing his injured shoulder. Katherine was fast asleep on the sofa. My mother, by now unfazed by anything that happens during the Clifton Hampden weekend, asked Duncan if he would like a nice cup of tea.

My own 'Roger moment' came when I had made the mistake of inviting Tom, an old friend in every sense of the word, to a game. I was batting when he decided to help out with the umpiring. I had advanced into double figures for the first time in years at Clifton Hampden and was feeling good. I felt sure that the illusive Clifton Hampden 50 was within my grasp, even though I was only on 12.

There was a half-hearted appeal from the bowler as the ball hit my pads. No one else appealed. I strolled nonchalantly out of my crease to pat down the pitch six inches outside my leg stump when I noticed Tom pointing his finger in the air. Thinking that he had spotted a red kite or something, I looked up in the sky only to realise that he was in fact indicating that, in his opinion, I was out.

As I trudged despondently off, the wicket keeper

- a decent sort - said 'did you hit it Mike?' I realised at that moment, I had been taken to the top of a mountain, or more likely Wittenham Clumps, and was being tempted. If I said yes, he would have called me back. If I said no then I would have to continue the long walk back to the pavilion. I hadn't touched it so I couldn't say yes. That was it for another year.

'Cheating' in cricket is a grey area. In Test cricket, with the very odd exception, nobody walks for snicks to the keeper. In fact, some batsmen can be caught shoulder height at extra cover and still wait for the umpire's decision. If Freddie Flintoff knew he had nicked Brett Lee to the keeper, I wouldn't necessarily expect him to walk. But if Flintoff claimed a catch when he knew that he hadn't caught it, I'd be outraged even if the batsman was Matthew Hayden. Both actions could be described as cheating but one is accepted and the other isn't.

When I could bring myself to speak to Tom again - six months later - I asked him why he had given me out. He said that the ball hit my pad and he was pretty sure it would have hit the wicket. What can you say? Well, what I did say isn't printable in a family book but many of the words began with f and ended in g.

Needless to say, although Tom still turns up most years, I have never allowed him to umpire again. Usually when I am going out to bat he will accompany me on to the pitch with a white stick and pretend to take over from one of the umpires. He thinks this is hilarious. I thought it was mildly amusing the first time but still think what might have been all those years ago if the stupid bastard hadn't given me out.

Favourite umpiring story? Allan Lamb going out to bat

in a Test match and handing over his mobile phone to Dickie Bird saying sorry, he'd brought it out by mistake. Of course, he had left it on and Ian Botham rang it at the end of the over, asking if he could speak to Allan. Boys will be boys. Perhaps Inzamam should have tried it with Darrell Hair?

7. Simple Twist Of Fate

1981 was a memorable year for many reasons. Prince Charles and I got married, to Diana and Jill respectively. Ronald Reagan was elected President of the United States for the first time. Bucks Fizz won the Eurovision Song Contest and there were riots on the streets of Brixton. Apart from all happening in the same year, there is no obvious connection between these events but it might be fun to try and find one.

One of the other momentous events in 1981 was the Ashes series in general and the Headingley Test in particular. The 2005 Ashes win was fantastic but nothing, for me, has matched the excitement of the Headingley Test of 1981. It has become known as Botham's Test because of his extraordinary 149 not out when all seemed lost. But Australia only needed 130 to win in the second innings and someone had to bowl them out to win the match for England.

Bob Willis may not be everyone's cup of tea as a cricket commentator, indeed many people go and make a cup of tea when he is on, but anyone who changes his name from plain old Robert George Willis to Robert George Dylan Willis because he loves Bob Dylan so much, can't be that bad. He gave me more sustained, continuous pleasure on that Tuesday in July 1981 than any heterosexual man could give to another heterosexual man and still walk tall into his local the next day. He had me rolling on the floor in ecstasy.

To set the record straight, I should confirm that I really did get married in October of that year. No one should get married in the middle of the cricket season. Charles and Di did and look what happened to them.

It was a very warm July and it was the last day of the Headingley Test so I decided that, rather than do any real work, I would 'visit some customers'. This was in the glorious time before mobiles, email, bluetooth, blackberries and whatever. Before everyone had to be contactable 24/7, as the common vernacular has it (with the emphasis on common).

Anyway, back in 1981 there were no such worries. Just settle down and watch the cricket. The only way of contacting me was by the normal telephone but as I wasn't supposed to be there, I didn't have to answer it. Botham and Willis had been not out overnight but with only 4 runs added, Willis was out and Australia needed a mere 130 to win. At 56-1 things didn't look good but an inspired Bob soon had the Australians reeling.

As each wicket fell, I was one step closer to heaven and when Bright was yorked by Willis, I collapsed in a heap on the carpet. Robert George Dylan Willis had taken 8 wickets for 43 runs in 15.1 overs and there was no direction home for the Australians. They were all out for 111.

Australians are superstitious about 'Nelson' and clearly with good reason. It probably originates from the 1954-5 series against England when they were all out for 111 twice and they eventually lost the series 3-1.

Nelson in cricket is 111, 222 is Double Nelson, 333 Triple Nelson and so on. So why is it called Nelson and why is it considered bad luck? Some Australians, perhaps with an incomplete grasp of British history, may think it refers to Admiral Lord Nelson because he was unlucky enough to only have one arm, one leg and one eye (111). However, Nelson did in fact have both legs, but was indeed missing an arm and the sight of one eye. Even so, he still had enough appendages to give the French a sound thrashing on more than one occasion and, as a student of history himself, probably gave them the two finger salute with his remaining arm, after each battle. This goes back to Henry V's days. When the French captured English soldiers, they would cut off two fingers on the right hand so they could not fire their longbows. At Agincourt, apparently the English bowmen all gave the two-finger sign to the French to show that they had all their digits. We have been doing it ever since.

A French statesman once said to Lord Palmerston 'if I wasn't French, I would wish to be English'. Palmerston replied; 'if I wasn't English, I would wish to be English'. An excellent response and so true. Actually, it's a shame that the French don't play cricket. They have got the weather for it and plenty of countryside for cricket grounds. Cricket tours to France would be much easier to organise than to India or Australia or the West Indies. Wine would be compulsory with cricket teas. If the French played, there would be massive EEC subsidies for cricket. Farmers would be paid to stop growing crops and convert their fields into cricket pitches. There would probably be cricket bat 'mountains'. No school or club would ever be short of equipment. Of course, the rules of cricket would have to be translated into French and all bowlers instructed to shout 'C'est comment?' when appealing. Although the thought of losing to the French at cricket is too awful to contemplate, beating them would be wonderful.

Another explanation for Nelson is that the number refers to three of Admiral Nelson's great naval victories against the French at Copenhagen, the Nile and Trafalgar thus giving won-won-won (111). Whatever the derivation, being on Nelson in cricket is considered unlucky for teams in general and Australians in particular. If we did play the French at cricket, no doubt the term Nelson would soon be deemed politically incorrect.

However, all is not lost. There is a way to counter the curse of Nelson. There is a Gloucestershire superstition that if the score reaches 111, all will be well if the rest of the team have their feet off the ground until the two batsmen at the crease score another run to get off 111. So there you have it, if the Australians had been prepared to hop about on one leg at Headingley then they would have got off 111 and who knows, might have gone on to win. Until he retired in 2005, one of the more eccentric sights in first class cricket was umpire David

Shepherd hopping about on one leg until the team batting got themselves off Nelson. If he'd been in the Australian dressing room in 1981, he'd have had them all hopping up and down till the cows came home.

As we only have one game a year, a fixture card for the Mike Harfield XI would be a bit of a luxury. Nevertheless, everyone needs to know when the match is so that they can avoid arranging weddings, holidays, christenings and so on. I adopt a fairly comprehensive approach in contacting people about the Clifton Hampden match. A Christmas card with the date of the next year's match. A letter in the spring with the averages attached. This used to be written and is now email for most. Rob resolutely refuses to go on email. He has a computer in his house, but it wasn't plugged in when I last saw it and I'm not sure it ever has been. I print off the email and post it to him. I usually get a reply from him well before most of the others on email.

Back in 1981, email was just a twinkle in Bill Gates' eye and everyone got a real letter. I would then follow up with a phone call for those that were potentially unreliable. Although Vernon had always turned up when he said he would, I felt that a phone call would do no harm.

The conversation that year went something like this:

Me: 'Hi Vernon, how's it going?'
Vernon: 'Great thanks.'
Me: 'Are you OK for the match this year?'
Vernon: 'Err, when is it?'
Me: 'It's on August 9th. Did you get my letter?'

Vernon: 'Oh, well I'm getting married on the 7th.'

Me, hesitantly: 'Well that's a Friday, the game is on the Sunday.'

Vernon, slight pause: 'OK, yeah, right I'll be there.'

Me, almost fainting from a combination of gratitude and respect: 'Great.'

I don't think I have ever admired someone as much as I admired Vernon at that moment. He wasn't joking. He really intended to play.

Vernon: 'Do you know anywhere we can stay?'

Me: 'Well The Barley Mow is good and it's close to the ground.'

Vernon: 'If you give me the number, I'll book us in.'

Sorted! Vernon was going to get married on Friday, spend his honeymoon at Clifton Hampden on Saturday and play cricket for us on the Sunday. What a star! He might be a bit tired when I brought him back for his second bowling spell but that was a risk I was prepared to take.

As it happened, Colin was also staying at The Barley Mow for the weekend and they both turned up to book in on the Saturday at the same time. To picture the scene, you have to appreciate that Vernon is black and his wife of 24 hours is white. Colin is also white and his girlfriend, later wife, is black. They were all standing at the reception of The Barley Mow. In 1981 you didn't get many black people in The Barley Mow or Clifton Hampden or indeed in Oxfordshire. It is not very different today. Back in 1981, the young girl behind the reception desk was decidedly flustered. Were they renegades from the Brixton riots? Was it against the law for black and white people to sleep in the same room? Should she call the manager? The police? Her mother?

Eventually it was all settled amicably and the pre-match preparations and wedding celebrations were able to start in earnest. The next day, Clifton Hampden won the toss and batted. We restricted them to 116 for 9 at tea. Convention had it that whoever batted first declared at tea so we only needed to get 117 to win. This we did comfortably, losing only 3 wickets. Vernon was batting at the end and hit the winning run. Ending the honeymoon with a bang you could say.

Life was good. We had won three matches in a row making it 3-3 in the series. England had won the Ashes that summer. I was getting married in October and although, unlike Vernon, I hadn't any plans to play cricket on the honeymoon, we were going to Barbados so you never know. Should I pack my kit just in case? Maybe just the box?

I waited until the second week of the honeymoon before suggesting that we went and did a bit of sight seeing in Bridgetown. Oh look, there's a cricket ground! Unfortunately, or perhaps fortunately, there was no Test match on but there was a local game so we watched that for a while, with Jill perhaps getting an inkling of what was in store over the next 25 years whenever cricket was mentioned.

It's extraordinary that Barbados, an island with a population of less than 300,000, could have produced Learie Constantine along with the three W's - Clyde Walcott, Everton

Weekes and Frank Worrell. Furthermore, Gary Sobers, Wes Hall, Charlie Griffith and Conrad Hunte, together with Worrell, were all members of that victorious 1963 touring side and all were born in Barbados. Later came Malcolm Marshall, Gordon Greenidge, Joel Garner, Desmond Haynes and a host of other lesser lights. All from a place with a population the size of Stoke-on-Trent.

Stoke was picked entirely at random and no insult is intended. Stoke has also produced its share of sporting legends, such as Stanley Matthews, Garth Crooks and Frank Bough. You may snort at the mention of Frank Bough but in his own way he was a legend. As for Garth Crooks, he is unique; at least we certainly hope so. Cricket players should hope and pray that he sticks with football. Answering questions from Garth could be worse than facing Shoaib Akhtar on a fast pitch. 'So, Andrew Flintoff, you took no wickets, you were out first ball in both innings and you've just lost the Ashes. How do you feel?'

Stoke also produced Robbie Williams and Anthea Turner but that conjures up images too horrible to think about.

8. Maggie's Farm

The 1980s was a strange decade in many ways. The England cricket team had nine different captains, not all at the same time although sometimes it seemed like that. Brearley, Botham, Brearley again, Fletcher, Willis, Gower, Gatting, Emburey, Cowdrey, Gooch and then Gower again were all given a go as England captain during the '80s. Henry Blofeld came up with this classic comment during England's amazing three-run win over Australia at the Melbourne Cricket Ground. It was the Fourth Test during England's 1982/83 Ashes tour under Bob Willis's notional captaincy 'England have at least nine captains out there, unfortunately Bob Willis isn't one of them.'

Against the West Indies in the 1988 home series, they tried four different ones - Gatting, Emburey, Cowdrey and Gooch. Mike Gatting lost the job in somewhat bizarre circumstances. The Sun revealed that a 'sex orgy' had taken place in the team hotel during the First Test. Shock! Horror! Gatting admitted that he had invited a barmaid back to his room but that no 'improper behaviour' had taken place. The selectors accepted this but sacked him anyway. How typical of Gatting. What is the point in inviting a barmaid back to your hotel bedroom if no 'improper behaviour' takes place? He probably thought she was just bringing him a plate of bacon sandwiches.

Emburey was tried for the Second and Third Tests but it was decided that he wasn't good enough. Who to turn to? Chris Cowdrey, son of Colin and godson of Peter May (Chairman of the selectors at the time) was the obvious choice. He looked out of his depth and, after he was injured in a county match following the Fourth Test, never played Test cricket again. Gooch took over for the last Test. England lost the series 4-0 (Gatting had managed a draw despite his distractions), which was actually an improvement on the two previous series against the West Indies, both of which were lost 5-0.

The only bright spot in 1988 was the one-day series, which England won 3-0 before the proper cricket began. The Texaco Trophy matches, as they were known in those days, produced a number of curiosities. First of all, Monty Lynch was chosen for England but no one was really sure why. Apparently, the selectors thought they heard Gatting shout, ' I must have Lynch'. In fact he had said, ' I must have lunch'. Poor old Monty was run out by Gatting for 0 in the first match, scored 2 in the second, 6 in the third and wasn't chosen again. Although the West Indies lost the third game, Courtney Walsh managed to bowl eleven overs for 11 runs and Geoff Boycott wasn't even playing. The other oddity was that the West Indies found Derek Pringle and Gladstone Small very difficult to master. Perhaps they were just lulling England into a false sense of security?

In those days, the one day matches were just an aperitif before the main meal of 5-day Test matches began. Nowadays, you can be halfway through your first course when the restaurant is closed and you are forced to go and eat seven hamburgers in a row. I sometimes wake up in the middle of the night with a nightmare vision of the future, where touring sides play eleven 20:20 matches followed by nine one day matches, with one 3-day Test match at the end of the tour. If the Test match ends in a draw, Steve Harmison has to bowl at a single stump to secure victory for England.

England won the Ashes in 1981, 1985 and 1987 but kept getting hammered by the West Indians. Indeed, England did not win a single Test match against the West Indies throughout the 1980s.

Meanwhile, Margaret Thatcher was trying to destroy the country in order to save it. In 1981, opinion polls indicated that she was the most unpopular Prime Minister in history. The only thing that kept her from being given an early bath was a deep-seated patriotism within the British people that dictates that the majority will support any leader if the country is at war. This even worked for Blair for a while but it does have its limits.

The Falklands War - what was that all about? Some remote islands, 8,000 miles away, full of sheep and penguins. Why go to war over them? For those readers who know little or nothing about the Falklands War, imagine some distant relatives that you haven't seen for quite a while and aren't particularly keen to see again. They ring up and say that their evil landlord is trying to take their house away from them. As you are their only living relative, could you come and help? You ask whether it is his house and they say, well yes it is but they have been squatting there for a number of years and surely that gives them certain rights, and anyway he's really evil. So you round up the family and at great cost in time, money and life, you go and give the evil landlord a good thumping. Everyone (well nearly everyone) rejoices and you are very popular.

Here is a note for politicians; the Armed Forces worked it out a long time ago. If you are going to invade somewhere, make sure it is a smallish place and make sure you win quickly. Contrast the United States very successful invasion of Grenada (133,000 sq. miles, population 90,000) in 1982 with the invasion of Iraq (169 million sq. miles, population 24 million). If Iran is next on the Americans' list, they should think again. It's a lot bigger than Iraq and has far more people. They should be looking at somewhere like Western Samoa or if they are feeling confident, perhaps the whole of Samoa. It doesn't really matter to the American public who is invaded as long as it is seen as a success. Ronald Reagan and his PR men had obviously worked this out before they invaded Grenada.

The Falklands was very risky because of the distance, the logistics, the climate and not really being sure which side the French were on. Also, the Queen's son might have been shot down which would have taken a bit of explaining. In fact, it was a good job that it was the Queen's son and not the Prime Minister's son. Mark Thatcher would probably have got lost, landed his helicopter in Buenos Aires and tried to sell some

Exocets to the Argentinians.

In the end it all turned out well for Margaret Thatcher and she was able to continue on her merry way. Privatisation, what a good wheeze that was. Basically, it was saying to people, this share is worth £100. You can buy it for £50 and a few weeks after you have bought it you can sell it again for £100. Oh, and by the way, you owned it in the first place all along. Later came the Poll Tax, which was not such a brilliant idea and, together with being savaged by a dead sheep, ultimately led to her downfall.

Her resignation in 1990 effectively meant she 'walked'. Unusual for a batsman, even more surprising for a politician. She had been hit on the pads in front of the stumps but didn't wait for the umpire's decision. As you would expect, all the opposition had appealed but unfortunately for her, so had many of her own side. If she had referred the decision to the third umpire who knows, she may have been given the benefit of the doubt.

The 1982 Clifton Hampden match saw the arrival of another Roger in the team and he is still playing in the fixture today. He had many of the attributes that we were looking for. He played with a straight bat, he was a wicketkeeper and, he not only had his own kit, he owned two sports shops as well. Roger was a proper cricketer, you could just tell. There was no doubt that he would strengthen the side immeasurably. He opened the batting for us and was immediately out for 1.

Cricket is different from any other sport in that if you make a mistake as a batsman, that can be it. Sometimes there is no second chance. A centre forward may miss an open goal but he is able to carry on playing and working for another opportunity. A golfer may miss a 3-foot putt but he can make up for it on the remaining holes. A tennis player puts an easy volley into the net and loses the set but he can still come back and win. But this was cricket and Roger's batting was over for the day before he had even got going. However, class will always prevail if you give it long enough and Roger has scored more runs in the Clifton Hampden fixture, over the years, than anyone else.

Back in 1982, nobody else scored many runs that day either and we subsided for the grand total of 103. Although we would have welcomed this number of runs a few years before, our expectations had been raised by three successive victories. 103 wasn't a big score and a glance at the scorebook had a déjà vu look about it. The dismissals included three LBWs and two run outs.

The Clifton Hampden scorebook, which I look after from one year to the next, has all our matches in it, starting from 1976. Ricky Gervais was once asked by a naive magazine interviewer what one thing he would take out of his flat if it was on fire and he had 10 seconds to get out. He replied 'one of the twins'. My answer would have to be the Clifton Hampden scorebook. Ricky Gervais was joking but the interviewer didn't realise it. For some time it was thought that he really did have twins. I, of course, am not joking.

Clifton Hampden had only used four bowlers, a far cry from those early matches when Geoff Boycott's grandmother would have been given a couple of overs if she had been playing and probably would have been quite successful. Defending a total of only 103 was going to be difficult and Clifton Hampden started confidently. However, once again Rob was inspired and, assisted by Vernon, he ripped the heart out of the Clifton Hampden batting. I brought myself on to 'clean up the tail'. Any non-cricketers still reading at this point would be forgiven for being a little bemused. This is nothing to do with pet hygiene. Rather it is what captains do when they see the chance of some cheap wickets. Clifton Hampden were bowled out for 65 and miraculously we were 4-3 up in the series.

Having won in 1979 for the first time, we had started the decade with three straight wins - 1980, 1981 and 1982. Although we didn't know it at the time, that was it, we had peaked. The slow inexorable decline started around 1983 when we just about scraped a draw.

So why carry on playing for another 25 years after you have got as good as you are going to get and you only have embarrassment, potential humiliation and certain injury to look forward to? A good question which deserves some examination. There are some people, like my friend Ken, who are not prepared to accept a reduction in personal standards. As soon as they see that their powers are on the wane they stop playing cricket and take up golf, or go on cruise ships, or play golf on cruise ships.

Sydney Barnes played professional cricket until he was 65. This means that he was being paid to play cricket for over 40 years! That seems a fine way to spend your life. He lived to be 94, so I'm inclined to think that he possibly gave up playing too soon. He probably wasn't quite as good at 55 as he was when he was 25 but that didn't stop him playing.

We aren't paid to play at Clifton Hampden but we do get a jolly good tea, usually provided by Jean, Owen's wife. As long as Clifton Hampden keeps inviting us, we will keep turning up. Our games during the rest of the 1980s were nearly always close, occasionally we even won, but we were never quite the same force again. For most of us, that didn't matter.

The Clifton Hampden match was the catalyst that enabled us all to get together at least once a year. By now, the team and its supporters of various shapes, sizes and ages were scattered around the country and in some cases, the world. We needed an excuse to meet up and what better excuse than a cricket match?

In fact, it's hard to think of another activity that lends itself to this sort of occasion. Football - a bit too strenuous and a fleet of ambulances would have to be on permanent standby. Tennis - rather too twee and just not the right setting. Rugby - would be amusing but not very realistic.

There's something about the rhythm and texture of a village cricket match that is unique. It has a symmetry and a pace all of its own - pub, first innings, tea, second innings, pub. At Clifton Hampden, the cricket is in perfect harmony with its surroundings. The oak trees, the corn fields, the white of the player's clothing set against the green of the grass, the blue of the sky and the red of the eyes. Spectators don't have to know anything about the game to appreciate the ambience of a Sunday village cricket match.

For those not watching the cricket, one of our WAGs often provided an alternative source of entertainment. She seemed to regard sunbathing as a competitive sport. If sunbathing had been an Olympic event, and who is to say it won't be one day, she would have been up there challenging for medals. It could well explain one or two of our dropped catches around that time, but not all of them.

One year in the early 80s, we had a visit from a Czechoslovakian porn star. One of the WAGs brought her cousin to the game and apparently she was an absolute stunner. I say 'apparently' not because I'm trying to be coy but simply because I do not recall it. Colin had to remind me that it happened. Here I think we have a clue to our decline as a cricket team. It would take more than a Czechoslovakian porn star (please note that this is Colin's description not mine since I don't even remember seeing her) to deflect my attention from the cricket, but clearly the same cannot be said of the rest of the team.

The England cricket team had distractions of their own in the mid 1980s. Before the Sun had come up with the inventive but highly implausible idea of implicating Mike Gatting in a sex scandal, Ian Botham had been the usual tabloid target. On the 1986 tour of the West Indies Botham was allegedly involved with sex (breaking a bed with an ex-Miss Barbados), drugs (liberal use of cocaine, cannabis and heroin) and rock 'n' roll (parties with Mick Jagger). Only one of these was actually true (Mick does like his cricket) but when has the News of the World ever let the truth spoil a good story? It didn't help that England were getting hammered by the West Indies on the field. Another 'blackwash' was completed in Antigua with Viv Richards scoring a century off 56 balls

Botham had more problems to deal with when he got home in the spring of 1986. He had a long running legal dispute with the Mail on Sunday over alleged drug taking and other high jinks on an earlier tour to New Zealand. His personal manager - the eccentric and bizarre Tim Hudson - hadn't really helped by telling everyone that of course Botham smoked marijuana. Eventually, the dispute was settled with Botham giving a story to the Mail on Sunday in which he admitted to smoking the odd joint from time to time. The headline writers had a field day. 'Botham does it on grass' and 'Botham goes to pot' to name but two.

The TCCB was outraged and he was banned from first class cricket until the end of July. I refused to join in the general condemnation. Although this is my first book, I have been published before. I wrote this searing indictment of the cricket authorities and it won £5 as letter of the week in the Birmingham Daily News.

Sir - 'England without Botham is like Benson without Hedges, port without cigars, Sunday without John Players, gin without tonic, the MCC without humbug.'

That showed them.

Without him, England lost the three match series to India 2-0, and lost one and drew one of the first two Tests against New Zealand. Botham meanwhile scored 175 not out, including thirteen 6s, in a John Player Sunday League game for Somerset when he was finally allowed to play again. He was recalled to the England team for the last Test against New Zealand at the Oval. True to his script, he took a wicket with his first ball, thus equalling Dennis Lillee's world record for Test wickets (becoming the joint world record holder you could say) and then another in his third over to beat it. For good measure he scored 50 off 32 balls when England batted before rain ensured that the game would be a draw. Botham hadn't made a hash of it; he was back with a hit.

During the 1980s Colin and I both played cricket for Snaresbrook CC in Wanstead. For a few glorious years, we finally did what we should have been doing since leaving school - playing cricket twice every weekend. We managed to persuade Rob to play a few games and even Clive turned out a couple of times when the carp weren't biting. In pursuit of my dream of having a really fast West Indian bowling attack against Clifton Hampden, I once asked Rikki to play for us. Rikki was a bit older than us, played for the first team at Snaresbrook and was a really good player. He was West Indian, pretty cool, pretty pacey when he wanted to be and also a decent bat. Perfect for the Clifton Hampden match.

He seemed keen to play even though it was about an hour and a half drive from Northeast London to Clifton Hampden. I thought that the directions I gave him were fairly clear but as 2.30 approached, things did not look good. I left instructions at the Plough that if a West Indian turned up - any West Indian - then they should direct him to the cricket ground. Rikki never did make it. Fortunately, I had lined up a reserve who, through no fault of his own, wasn't West Indian but at least he was there.

When I asked Rikki, the following week, why he hadn't made it, he claimed to have got lost on the North Circular. Now the North Circular was a hell of a road, particularly before the

M25 was finished, but to get lost on it is quite difficult. Come off it too soon - yes, go the wrong way round it - maybe, but get lost on it? Looking back, I think that he originally agreed to play one Saturday night after a game and after a couple of beers. My enthusiasm for his participation obviously lasted much longer than his own.

It's amazing what you can get people to agree to after a game of cricket and a few beers. At least two Mike Harfield XI tours of the West Indies have been planned in the aftermath of a Clifton Hampden match but sadly have not yet materialised. There's still time!

9. The Times They Are A-Changin'

It was hard to believe at the time, and it's somehow even harder to believe now, but John Major was Prime Minister from 1990 to 1997. Incredibly, he was one of the few people ever to hold the offices of Foreign Secretary, Chancellor of the Exchequer and Prime Minister. Not bad for a poor boy from Brixton who left school at 16 with three O-levels and, what's more, he was a self-confessed 'cricket nut'. You can just imagine Margaret Thatcher telling him off in Cabinet meetings for whispering the Test score to Kenneth Clarke. 'Major! Stay behind afterwards!'

Yet there was always something not quite right about John Major. It wasn't his fault that his father had a failed garden gnome business or that people thought that he tucked his shirt into his underpants. It wasn't really his fault that he was in charge on Black Wednesday when the country lost hundreds of millions of pounds, destroying the Tory image of economic competence. And it certainly wasn't his fault that his son married a Sun Page 3 girl. The Labour MP, Tony Banks, summed it up when he said of Major in 1994 that 'He was a fairly competent chairman of Housing [on Lambeth Council]. Every time he gets up now I keep thinking, 'What on earth is Councillor Major doing?' I can't believe he's here and sometimes I think he can't either.'

Nowadays, John Major is probably best remembered for getting back to basics with Edwina Currie. When their four-year 'fling' was revealed to the nation by Edwina in her own personal interpretation of the Freedom of Information Act, Major said, 'It is the one event in my life of which I am most ashamed.' What? More than rail privatisation? More than allowing councils to sell off all the school cricket pitches? Surely not.

If you have a really hot vindaloo, you may enjoy it at the time but you invariably regret it the next morning. Would you keep going back to the same restaurant each week for four years and have the same dish? I don't think so.

The Clifton Hampden match continued through the 1990s. We secured an occasional draw but usually we lost. During this time we managed to score 222 one year and contrived to lose and 212 the next year and only drew. Both times, Clifton Hampden were 8 wickets down but we couldn't finish them off.

What was the problem? Why couldn't we win anymore? There were lots of possible reasons:

1. The opposition was getting younger.
2. We were getting older.
3. Our bowling attack had developed Trueman like qualities but unfortunately it was more [2]Christine than Fred.
4. Our fielding, once athletic, was now bordering on arthritic.
5. The sun was in our eyes.
6. The captain was crap.

The last two are obviously jokes and not real reasons why we couldn't win.

What was to be done? We couldn't rely on a Russian billionaire coming along to inject new blood into the team and anyway, it would destroy the 'spirit' of the fixture if we had lots of people in the team who were really good at cricket. No, we had to rely on the youth policy that many of us had invested heavily in over the years.

Our WAGs had done their best to help by producing nine [3]SOPs over the years but when would they be ready? And when they were ready, would they like playing cricket? And if they liked playing cricket, would they want to play with a bunch of old farts?

There also had to be some vacancies in the team. The old rule of 'if you play one year and are available the next, then you are in' still applied. This proved to be less of a problem than I imagined. Hugh was the first to bow to the inevitable. In 1066, William the Conqueror had ordered his men to drill holes in the bottom of their boats when they landed from Normandy. This was to show them that there was no going back and thus

---

2   I know it's spelt Truman, don't be pedantic.
3   Sons of Players

make them fight harder. It seemed to work! In 1996, in a similar vein, Hugh announced that he had taken his cricket kit to the local Oxfam shop. He was retiring from cricket and did not want to be tempted back, ever.

This was a great shame, not just from a cricketing point of view but from a sartorial one too. Hugh's dress sense had become increasingly eccentric over time and what he would be wearing was always a highlight to look forward to each year. His Adam Ant New Romantic look was a personal favourite of mine but I think it was his Rupert Bear trousers that took first prize for most people. Sadly, Hugh hasn't been to the Clifton Hampden matches for a while. He has become somewhat of a recluse and seems to be setting up his own Trappist monk sect somewhere in North Wales. I know where it is but he'd never talk to me again if I told you.

Rob, Hugh's fellow opening bowler, was not the force of old and, as each year went by, I noticed him looking wistfully at the cricket club bar and the spectators sprawled round the boundary sipping a cold beer. It seems that he had become disenchanted with the idea of having a hard cricket ball hit at him or thrown at him when he could be having a beer on the boundary and chatting to old mates. I must say I found it surprisingly difficult to put up any reasoned argument against this point of view.

However, whereas Hugh had retired, never to don the whites again, Rob said that he would always be there, with his kit, and if I ever needed him, he would play. Such loyalty and commitment almost brought a tear to my eye.

Having lost contact with Vernon sometime in the 1980s

- the person that answered his phone sounded very suspicious of my polite enquiries as to his whereabouts - our opening attack that had seen us through the glory years was now all but defunct.

We needed a new hero. Who would put their hand up? Who would stand up and be counted? Step up to the plate? Come to the party? I had tried to take the positives out of our ten years without a win but we just weren't putting the ball in the right areas. We always took one game at a time but now we wanted the bragging rights. (Please stop. Ed)

Although Steve had lived in Munich since the early 1980s, he hadn't missed a match - and still hasn't. Up to the point of delivering the ball, Steve looked a bit like Bob Willis coming off his slow run or at least Graham Gooch doing an impersonation of Bob Willis coming off his slow run. Regrettably, the similarity ended there. Once the ball left his hand, Steve didn't really know what it was going to do, but then nor did the batsman. Steve played league cricket but unfortunately it was the Munich ex-pat league made up of six teams of itinerant Europeans, with the odd Australian thrown in. Steve and I, from being second or third change, were now the cutting edge of our bowling attack. Some clue to our inability to win a match for over ten years is contained within the previous sentence.

In 1996, we batted first and scored a very creditable 208-8. After tea, Clifton Hampden were soon 40 for no wicket. It looked like the familiar pattern was going to repeat itself. I had opened the bowling with Steve and had been hit all over the place. I took myself off aiming to come back for some cheap wickets towards the end. Colin took my place. He had played in every game since 1976 and the opposition were familiar with his bowling technique. Imagine, if you can, Inzamam-ul-Haq bowling in the style of Shane Warne. Colin is probably the slowest bowler in the history of cricket. It is impossible to truly describe how slow he is, you have to see it to believe it. From the moment he bowls, the batsman has time to take his guard, do up his laces, have a cup of tea and discuss the weather with the wicket keeper before the ball actually arrives. The general reaction of batsmen is to get very excited and smash the ball a very long way.

The only advantage that Colin has is that if the batsman ever makes the mistake of letting the ball land on the pitch, it can turn quite significantly. On this occasion, as the batsman was trying to decide whether to hit the first ball for a six or a four, it pitched outside the leg stump, turned about a foot and clean bowled him. Rather like Mike Gatting after Shane Warne's 'ball of the century' at Old Trafford in 1993, the batsman left bemused, smiling and shaking his head and we had our first breakthrough. The new batsman departed immediately in a similar manner and Clifton Hampden were 40-2. The next batsman did not let the ball pitch once and hit four boundaries in succession. Then he skied one and the catch was taken. 56-3!

Just as I was thinking it was safe to bring myself back on, Steve got a wicket, then another, then another, and then another. He took the last seven wickets and ended up with 7-44. We had found our new hero. It was a purple patch that would have made Prince green with envy. Four of his victims were clean bowled and Clifton Hampden were all out for 85. We had won a match for the first time for 10 years. Was this a renaissance or a false dawn? Only time would tell.

Steve was referred to as 'Golden Arm' for at least a week afterwards. You can tell that we aren't a proper cricket team because we don't have nicknames. Rob is called Rob, Clive is called Clive and Duncan is called Duncan (except by Roger who usually refers to him as that stupid Scottish bastard (see earlier chapter on umpiring). Ray has always been called 'Reg' by Rob but no one, including Rob, knows why. Nobody else calls him that so it doesn't really count.

In first class cricket, nicknames are virtually mandatory. Usually it entails adding a 'y' as in Vaughny or Inzy or Thorpey (also known, rather more surprisingly, as 'The Shagger'). Sometimes it can be wittier as in 'Pica' (Graham Dilley) or 'Creepy' (John Crawley.) or 'Dizzy' (Jason Gillespie). Occasionally it is positively inspired as in 'Afghanistan' (the forgotten war) when Mark Waugh couldn't get in the Australian team. And of course the commentators all have nicknames - 'Dave Gower, Beefy, Bumble, Mick and Titch', or something like that. Not forgetting Michael Holding aka 'the Whispering Death' who has yet to come up with an equivalent bon mot to Brian Johnston's memorable 'The bowler's Holding, the batsman's Willey'.

Football nicknames are usually even more banal than cricket ones but someone at Spurs had an inspired moment when Justin Edinburgh was nicknamed 'Musselburgh' (because, Musselburgh is just in Edinburgh). Geddit? The same goes for football chants which usually range from the crass to the obscene to the tedious and back again.

One chant, however, that never actually saw the light

of day was brilliant. Someone apparently thought that it would be a good idea for Millwall to play a 'friendly' with the Iranian national team. 'Millwall friendly' is almost the perfect example of an oxymoron, with the emphasis on moron. Before international relations could be irreparably damaged, common sense prevailed and the match was called off but not before the Millwall fans had prepared the following chant. 'You're Shiite, and you know you are'.

Millwall fans coming up with an intelligent, witty football chant. Whatever next? It is a bit of a shock when your life-long prejudices are turned upside down. Like finding out that Mark Thatcher doesn't have pictures of William Zantzinger on his bedroom wall and is in fact a deeply sensitive individual who gives all his money to charity. Or discovering that Rupert Murdoch is actually a really nice bloke and a good guy to sit down and have a beer with.

For a while, I held the faintly ludicrous notion that, by not having Sky, I was making a stand against Murdoch's ever advancing, all embracing, evil media empire. With so much sport on Sky, this principled position clearly was not tenable for long. How to resolve it? Simon Barnes is one of my favourite sports journalists and, luckily, I was able to persuade myself that as he had taken the Murdoch shilling, by writing for The Times, then it was OK for me to have Sky.

Here's another cricket question for the pub (no checking on the internet). The Sky commentary team is sitting round the table. Sir Ian Botham (greatest English all rounder since W.G.), Mike Atherton (115 Tests and the best batsman of his generation, if you don't count Mark Ramprakash), David Lloyd (amateur stand up comedian from Accrington and ex umpire) and Nasser Hussain (96 Tests and ex England captain). Which one has the highest individual Test score?

The answer of course is David Lloyd - Bumble to his mates. He scored 214 not out against India in 1974. He then went on the 1974/75 tour of Australia and, along with most of the batsmen, was blown away by Thomson and Lillee. He only played 9 Tests for England but finished with an average of just over 42, higher than all three of his esteemed colleagues.

If David Gower had joined the table he could boast a top score of only one more than Bumble - his 215 against Australia in 1985. For the record, Atherton's top score was 185 not out against South Africa in 1995, Nasser Hussain scored 207 against Australia at Edgbaston in 1997 and Botham hammered India for 208 in 1982. So Athers never made a Test double century (presumably because 5 days wasn't long enough) and Jason Gillespie did. Funny old game cricket.

10. Things Have Changed

'Purer than pure' Labour were elected in 1997, partly because of the perceived 'sleaze' of the previous Tory administration. Within months, Tony Blair was trying to explain that Bernie Ecclestone had given the Labour Party £1 million out of the goodness of his heart and in no way did it influence the decision to exclude Formula One from the ban on all tobacco sponsorship in sport. As Tony said; 'I'm a pretty straight sort of guy.' Yeah, right. Whatever.[4]

That year, a waterlogged pitch meant we couldn't play our match at Clifton Hampden, the only time rain has prevented the game from taking place. Despite this, or some might say because of it, more people than usual turned up and we had a

---

4   You might think that this is not a particularly sophisticated political observation but really 'Yeah, right. Whatever' just about says all you need to say.

great weekend. On the Sunday afternoon, once it was confirmed that there wasn't going to be any cricket, we played a 14-a-side game of football. Over the years, many of us had played for a football team called 'The Flying Pigs'. The team had got its name from Rob's style of playing football, which was loosely based on his rugby playing days as a hooker in Sunderland. His robust approach to football was well suited to the killing fields of Wanstead Flats where 'The Flying Pigs' could be seen plying their trade, indeed it was actively encouraged. Rob is a stranger to compromise and felt no compunction in demonstrating the art of the airborne, two-footed tackle at our kickabout at Clifton Hampden. The 12-year-old on the receiving end was surprised to say the least.

One bonus of not playing cricket was that for the first time, the players were able to sample my mother's tea. Each year, while the team has tea in the pavilion with the Clifton Hampden players, everyone else goes back to my mother's house for tea. It is an open secret that many people only come to the match for her tea. After the game, many spectators have no idea what happened in the cricket but can tell you in detail what they had for tea. This is not to diminish the Clifton Hampden cricket tea, which was always suspiciously appetising, especially if we were fielding second, but my mother spends months preparing enough cakes and sandwiches to make a combination of Cyril Smith, Robbie Coltrane and Mike Gatting cry 'Enough!'

In 1998, normal service was resumed in every sense. With totally unfounded confidence, I chose to bat first and we struggled to a total of 132. It was not nearly enough, especially when 'Golden Arm' Steve's first 4 overs went for 39. We were stuffed by 8 wickets and the answer to the 'renaissance or false dawn' question was becoming a little clearer. We had two SOPs playing for us but they weren't quite ready to take on the massive responsibility of carrying an ageing team - in some cases literally as in most games someone pulled a hamstring or strained a calf muscle and had to be helped off the field.

Things looked as though they were going from bad to worse the following year. For the first time, I was really struggling to get a team together. Colin, showing a worrying lack of commitment and a mystifying sense of priorities, couldn't play as he was taking his son to a cricket match in Leeds.

John, a friend from work, had played the previous year, as had his oldest son, Jack. John had wanted his other son, Ross, to play this year as well. I was reassured by the information that Ross had played for Surrey under 16s but was more than a little concerned by the following telephone conversation just two weeks before the game.

Me: 'Hi John. Everything OK for Clifton Hampden?'
John: 'Oh, I'm glad you rang. I'm afraid Ross can't make it.'
Me (calmly): 'That's a shame. What's up?'
John: 'He's got rugby training.'
Me (incredulously): 'What? In June?'
John: 'It's with the England under 16 squad.'
Me: 'That's all very well but this is the Clifton Hampden match.'
John: 'Sorry.'
Me: 'At least you and Jack are OK to play?'
John: 'I'm afraid I have to take Ross to the rugby.'

Me: 'So how is Jack going to get to Clifton Hampden?'
John: 'He can't make it either I'm afraid.'
Me (forgetting that I had rung him): 'Well thanks for letting me know.'

As an experienced cricket captain by now, I was used to phone calls like this but not one that deprived me of three players at a stroke with only two weeks to go before the match. What to do?

First of all Rob was called out of retirement (it wouldn't be the last time). I had already enlisted my eldest son, John. He was 16, hadn't played much cricket but was keen to have a game. With the weekend fast approaching I had no choice but to ask, and if necessary, beg David, my 14 year old, to play. Apart from in the garden and on the beach, he had never played any cricket and had showed little inclination to do so. He soon saw how desperate I was and played hard to get but eventually agreed to turn out. That left one more to get. My third son, Tim, was 8 and enthusiastic. Tempting but there could be awkward discussions with his mother if he got hit by the ball. He was just a bit too young. (Tim eventually made his debut a few years later as a substitute for the only thing most of the team could pull these days - a hamstring.) I still needed one more player!

Bob was a friend of mine because a trainee dentist failed his exams in 1971 and had to move out of the Shepherds Bush flat I was in when I first lived in London. Bob answered the advert in Guy's Hospital and moved into the flat. We had been friends ever since and he'd never missed a Clifton Hampden match. Up to now he had always been on the spectator side of the boundary. As far as I knew, he had never played cricket in his life. Fast approaching 50, I felt that it was high time he did. I soon discovered that playing cricket wasn't on his 'things to do before I die' list. 18-year-old Swedish twins (female) and slender-billed curlews (male or female) both featured strongly but not necessarily at the same time or in that order.

I said that I'd see what I could do about the Swedish twin thing and would definitely let him know if I saw a slender-billed curlew, so he agreed to play on condition that he didn't have to use Colin's box. We had eleven players!

As I went out for the pre-match toss with the Clifton Hampden captain, I suggested that it might be a good idea if they batted first. I told him that we were 'a little weak' this year but didn't go into any more detail. Most captains prefer to bat first and he readily agreed. We bowled and fielded OK but predictably enough, they made hay in the sunshine and declared at tea on 234-5.

It would not be an exaggeration to say that I was a little worried about our batting line up. The tail started with me and I was batting at No.4. The chances of scoring 235 runs was as likely as Glenn McGrath predicting an England Ashes' win and holding out for a draw seemed nearly as likely as Mike Gatting turning down the offer of an extra cream bun.

Roger, the wicket keeper and most reliable batsman in the team, gave us a good start but, once he was out, the innings subsided. Seven wickets were down for about 130 runs and there were still 10 overs to go. At this point, my eldest came in. With the abandon of youth, and frankly not realising how difficult batting really is, he scored 20-odd runs and got the spectators' attention in a way that the rest of us had failed to do in the previous 23 years. Usually, only my mother watched the game with any interest but now everyone's focus was on the play. With two overs to go the eighth wicket fell and David joined his elder brother.

Aged 14, and playing in his first ever game of cricket, the odds were against him. Somehow he not only survived but, by swiping the ball over all the fielders crowded round him, managed to score 6 runs as well. He was out on the last ball of the match, trying to hit a six but missed the ball and demolished his stumps instead. Bob had been deprived of a hero's entrance. He'd been padded up for half an hour waiting to make his lifetime batting debut. It wasn't to be but his very presence had saved the day. Had he not been there, with no one left to go in, we would have lost. As it was, at 177-9, we had salvaged a draw and honour was satisfied on all sides.

I was very grateful to David for stepping into the breach that year, and a couple of other times in later years, but I couldn't help thinking that I had failed as a father. He really wasn't very keen on cricket. How could that have happened?

He had been given the cricket bat for Christmas, the Wisden for his birthday, the bedtime stories of Geoffrey Boycott's greatest innings, the two hours compulsory nets after school and the special treat of going to see Michael Atherton bat out all day for a draw at Old Trafford. Where did I go wrong?

I had been converted to cricket at an early age. As a boy, I had been a Yorkshire county cricket supporter. There, I've admitted it; I'm out of the closet and I feel a lot better for it. Furthermore, from the age of 11 to 13, I kept a scrapbook of

Yorkshire cricket newspaper cuttings. Well, there wasn't much to do in the evenings back then. You don't get boys doing that sort of thing these days do you? Come to think of it, you didn't get many doing it when I was young.

I stopped when I was 13, which is a shame. My social life didn't really improve much until I was about 20, so I could have quite easily carried on for another seven years. I would have had a rich source of county reports and other cricket material to help while away the hours waiting for the Ashes TV coverage to start in Australia. The cuttings I do have give some fascinating glimpses of a past age, such as this description of Fred Trueman batting for Yorkshire against the West Indies in 1963. 'Trueman had already embarked on another well organised innings to the contentment of a crowd of 8,000. As a brother fast bowler he was, of course, spared the fears that Griffith might be going to drop one short and he played with much authority until the declaration.' How times change.

I only supported Yorkshire because my father did. Why he supported them, having been born in Berkshire and never having lived in Yorkshire, is somewhat of a mystery. I think it may have had something to do with the fact that Yorkshire used to be the Manchester United, or Liverpool if you like, of county cricket. Since the County Championship began, they have won the title 30 times. Of the other counties, only Surrey have come close with 18 titles.

When I was putting my scrapbooks together in the 1960s, cricketers were nearly always referred to only by their surname. The tabloids would call Trueman 'Fiery Fred' but the 'sensible' papers with proper match reports would invariably use only surnames. The county section in Wisden might say Brian Close as he was the captain but everyone else was Binks or Boycott or Illingworth.

Consequently, the initials of the Yorkshire players became significant to me. It was D.E.V. Padgett rather than Doug and P.J. Sharpe instead of Phil. Initials have always been important in cricket. The most famous cricketer ever is immediately recognisable as W.G. and the player who would like to be the most famous cricketer ever is known as K.P., presumably because he's nuts. Nice one Kev!

Until the early 60s, a distinction was made between amateurs (The Gentlemen) and professionals (The Players). The last Gentlemen v Players game was in 1962. Until that point, scorecards at Lords always showed amateurs with their initials before their surname and professionals after. When Fred Titmus made his professional debut at Lords as a sixteen-year-old, he was no doubt put at his ease by a loudspeaker announcement apologising for an error on the printed scorecard. "F.J. Titmus' should read 'Titmus F.J.'."[5]

These things are important. Once amateurs and professionals started sharing the same changing room and the initials differentiation was dropped, it was but a short step to the loss of the Empire and coloured advertising slogans painted on the outfield.

---

5   Source: 'A Social History of Cricket' by Derek Birley

11. Most Of The Time

The new millennium started hilariously with the Blairs inviting the Windsors and the Prescotts over to the Millennium Dome for a New Year's Eve party. At midnight, everyone apart from the Queen crossed arms and sang the traditional rendition of Auld Lang Syne. You can't really blame her. Just when you want to spend a quiet evening with family and friends, some arriviste insists that you join him to celebrate 1,000 years of civilization in truly vulgar style. The Queen did however just about hold hands with Tony Blair, the first recorded instance of royalty touching a commoner since Prince Philip clipped a grouse beater round the ear for sneezing as he was about to shoot.

The first Clifton Hampden match of the new millennium was something of an anti-climax. With four SOPs in the side, we fielded and bowled pretty well, restricting the opposition to 169. Opening the bowling for Clifton Hampden was a player with a disconcerting resemblance to Shoaib Akhtar. He hadn't played against us before so, as I was starting the umpiring, I asked about him. The reply came back: ' He's just joined this season.' Fair enough. 'He plays for us on Saturdays.' Alarm bells start ringing. 'He's quite useful.' Oh dear.

He was indeed 'quite useful'. Another accurate bit of information would have been 'bloody quick'. He took 4 wickets for 7 runs in his first three overs. I don't think the concept of Sunday friendly was familiar to him. Fortunately the captain took him off and we staged a bit of recovery. He came back later bowling slow off breaks and finished with 6 for 16. We were all out for 95, the first time we hadn't reached three figures for many a year. If someone is a really good bat then he can play in fixtures like ours, enjoy himself and score lots of runs. Apart from perhaps giving the bowlers some embarrassing figures, he isn't going to wreck the game for everyone else. The trouble with being a really good bowler, especially a fast one, is that you can spoil the game if you end up bowling at batsmen who are just not good enough to see the ball let alone hit it. It wasn't his fault; he just turned up at the wrong game. He was a good bloke but mercifully he hasn't played against us again.

The next year it transpired that if Clifton Hampden progressed to the county cup competition semi-final (unlikely), and were drawn at home (a 50:50 chance), and the game was postponed because of rain, then the Sunday we were due to play was potentially a designated date for a cup match replay. The chances were about as high as being able to distinguish Ant from Dec or the Liberal Democrats banning sandals from their next annual Party Conference.

As luck would have it, Clifton Hampden did get through to the semi-finals, were drawn at home and did have the game rearranged for 'our' date. It was a fixture secretary and captain's nightmare. As I was both, it was a double whammy but no one asked for my resignation. Everyone seemed to enjoy the weekend and many of the people barely seemed to notice that we didn't play any cricket.

The following year, with the help of a 'friend of a friend' who scored an effortless fifty and some runs from Colin, who returned as the prodigal son but not with his own prodigal son, we scored 208. We were one wicket short of bowling Clifton Hampden out at the end of day.

One of the wickets was a run out by a throw from deep mid wicket by the same 'friend of a friend' who scored fifty. I needed to get to know him better, find out when his birthday was, maybe send him a Christmas present. When I tried to get him to play the following year it turned out that he was about to go to a jungle in central Africa on a two-year study of wild life. According to Rob there is a lot of that in Sunderland so there really wasn't any need to go quite so far away. Although I said that we would have a whip round for a return airfare to enable him to come back and play, he didn't take me up on my offer. Just when I had found a genuine 'ringer' who actually turned up, God or fate had taken him away.

God certainly does move in mysterious ways. When a golfer, usually American, attributes his win to God, you can't help but marvel at God's attention to detail. He's prepared to take time out from all the big issues that He has to deal with - war, famine, pestilence and so forth - to help a golfer sink a five foot putt. Why He helps one golfer to win rather than another, when they are both praying to Him, is not entirely clear. Seemingly, He increasingly helps some Premiership footballers - Portsmouth actually have a prayer meeting before the match - so He really is kept pretty busy. I'm never quite sure what the deal is when the goalkeeper asks God to help him stop goals and the centre forward on the other side asks God to help him score goals. It must be quite a quandary. It's a whole new subject for paranoiac football managers to exploit. Expect a rant from a Premiership manager any day now about God not being fair to both sides. Apparently God told George W Bush to invade Iraq and it's well known that Tony Blair has a personal direct line to both of them. Well God asked me to write this. 'Bush is a simple minded, religious fanatic and Blair is a sanctimonious git.' Sorry if this offends anyone but God told me to write it. No really, He did.

Time to get back to the cricket I think. We have continued to put out a decent team each year and have always made a respectable fist of the match, although we haven't actually won since Golden Arm Steve's heroic performance in 1996. With six of the team from the early days still playing, we usually need a few SOPs in the side for the sake of the fielding if nothing else. As players 'mature', it is generally the fielding that finds you out first. Batting is usually OK unless someone is a bit quick (i.e. above slow medium). With bowling, you should be able to cope for a few overs, albeit at a reduced speed. Of course if you couldn't bowl a length to begin with, getting older isn't going to help.

It's the fielding where the SOPs really come into their own. By some strange law of physics, as you get over thirty, the ground seems to get further away and consequently, it takes you longer to get down to it. When you do eventually bend down to try and stop the ball, invariably it is either past you or it hits you. If you do manage to stop it properly, it is a certainty that your back / hamstring / Achilles tendon will protest at the unnecessary exertion it is being put through. SOPs don't have this problem yet but their time will come, even though it is inconceivable to them at the moment that they will ever be as clapped out as their fathers are.

The availability of the 'senior' players these days is more or less directly related to their performance in the game they have just played. Score a few runs or take a couple of wickets and it's; 'Of course I'm OK for next year.' 'Shame we don't play more often'. 'Tour? Great idea. Where shall we go?' Out for 0 or pull a muscle and it's; 'I think that's it. You can't play forever.' 'I just can't see the ball anymore.' 'Why don't we play golf instead?'

The SOPs of course don't have these moments of self-doubt but cannot be totally relied upon. Excuses for non-availability have ranged from girlfriend's graduation, to best mate's 21st, to gap year in Australia. Only the latter can really be considered a good enough reason for missing the Clifton Hampden match and even that is debatable.

My sister, Jane, has two potential SOPs but she made the mistake of marrying a non-cricketer and compounded the error by going to live in Scotland. Her children can't therefore in reality be considered for selection. She only manages to make the Clifton Hampden match about once every 10 years - a disturbing lack of commitment. It's only an 8 hour car journey. I really don't see what the problem is.

My other sister, Sue, has been to every Clifton Hampden match despite at various times being seven months pregnant and moving to live in Ireland (not in the same year). She has done her bit by producing two sons but they also are not included in the nine potential SOPs that I can, in theory, select from. The reason for this is that, some years ago, she took the extraordinary decision to marry a musician whose interest in cricket was similar to an atheist's belief in God. Her two boys seem to have inherited his genes. If I said to Patrick, go to third man, he would assume that I was talking about Orson Welles, and Alex playing air guitar at deep mid off would not alleviate our fielding problems.

All was not lost though. Through her work, Sue had got to know Andy Lloyd, the ex-England and Warwickshire player. Andy Lloyd had opened the batting for England against the West Indians in 1984 and they never got him out. Unfortunately for him, he was hit on the head by Malcolm Marshall in the first innings of his first Test. He retired hurt and never played for England again. As a consolation, his 8 not out gave him a Test batting average of infinity! By the time Sue got to know him, he'd had twenty years to recover, so I had high hopes of adding him to the squad. It also turned out that he was a friend of Ian Botham. Sue met them both through Botham's Pro-celebrity golf event that she organised at the Ring of Kerry Golf Club in Kenmare. My imagination was racing. Botham playing for the

Mike Harfield XI at Clifton Hampden.

I asked Sue what she was prepared to do to get Andy Lloyd and Ian Botham to play at Clifton Hampden. She said that she would buy them both a pint. It wasn't quite what I had in mind but it was a start. I had sleepless nights trying to decide where I should put Botham in the batting line up. Six was his favourite position but would he run out of partners too soon? I settled on four, batting myself at five to give him some experienced support in case he was nervous. I thought I would put Andy Lloyd at six so he wouldn't have to face the Clifton Hampden opening pace attack. Then there was the problem of when to bowl Botham; I decided probably first change rather than open with him. Finally, where to put him in the field? He would want to be at first slip but we had at least five others who wanted to field there and they did have seniority.

All my plans and concerns came to nothing. It transpired that both Andy Lloyd and Ian Botham were now golfers not cricketers, so even if I had been able to persuade Botham to break his Sky contract and 'throw a sicky', he would have turned up with his golf clubs instead of his cricket gear.

The Botham dream was over so instead we decided to have a party to celebrate 30 years of the Clifton Hampden cricket match. Sue's husband, Nick, couldn't help with the cricket playing but his band was going to provide the music. The best rock movie ever made is called 'The Last Waltz', which is a film of The Band's last concert. There is a multitude of guest appearances including Dylan, Neil Young, Eric Clapton, Van Morrison and many others. It's directed by Martin Scorsese and is a joyful celebration of all that is great about rock music.

I have had to check this twice but The Band's farewell concert actually took place in 1976, the year of the first Clifton Hampden cricket match. Time can play strange tricks. Our shindig was going to be a bit like 'The Last Waltz' except it wasn't a farewell. I had to be quite firm about this with some people. It was to be a celebration of our 30 years of cricket at Clifton Hampden with as many attending from both sides as possible.

It took place on the Saturday night with the usual match planned for the next day. Some of the individuals there had clearly seen better days and were only just able to stand unaided; but more about Nick and his band later. There was a good turnout from both sides but, although there were a lot of Clifton Hampden players, many of them no longer played against us. As most of our current team were present, and an early night was not on the cards, we could well be struggling when it came to the game the next day. Was I bothered? Well obviously, but strangely nobody else seemed to be.

Whereas five or six of our original team from the early days still played, none of the Clifton Hampden team did, so it was good to meet up with them again. Dave Bowden was also there. He had been at every match over the last 30 years, usually behind the club bar dispensing beer before, during and after the game. Dave is one of those guys that keeps cricket clubs like Clifton Hampden going and you wonder how they would survive without them. Each year he welcomes us and always seems genuinely pleased to see us all.

Somehow, over the years, I think we had inadvertently given the impression of being a slightly bohemian lot. It was true that Steve jetted in from Munich each year, and Hugh's dress sense was certainly unconventional but the reality was that we were a bunch of individuals thrown together by fate. If we tried hard, we could appear to be a little unorthodox, or in Hugh's case downright eccentric, but really we were just a group of friends with relatively conventional lives and a shared love of cricket.

The venue for the party was, appropriately enough, the Plough. Graham and Olwyn, who had recently taken over the pub, organised a marquee in the garden. Quite what Ken and Beryl, the previous owners, would have made of it all is anyone's guess. Music? ...Food? ...Fun? ...at the Plough?

Every generation from 8 to 80 was represented. Nick's band played some great music that managed to appeal to everyone. As someone who loves music but can't play an instrument to save my life, I am secretly in awe of musicians like Nick who can not only play all the right notes but in the right order as well. When the music is live, it adds an extra dimension to any occasion. And so it was at our 30 year Clifton Hampden bash. Children collapsed at regular intervals, not through an excess of alcohol, but through laughter at seeing their parents DANCING! The music went on into the night and I think it's fair to say that everyone enjoyed themselves.

We batted first the next day and somehow managed to score 187 but Clifton Hampden knocked the runs off for the loss of 7 wickets. The result didn't matter; well OK it did just a bit. What really mattered was that we had made it through 30 years and we were still going strong. The Rolling Stones continue to play rock concerts and Dylan is still on his Never

Ending Tour, so is there any reason why we shouldn't carry on playing cricket? This is a rhetorical question and I'm not really looking for an answer.

12. One More Weekend

The cricket World Cup in 2007 was arguably the most ponderous sporting event since, well since the last cricket World Cup. Even the Moldovan synchronised swimming trials for the Olympics were better organised and had more atmosphere. Just about everything that could go wrong did go wrong.

It seemed to go on forever! Actually, it was six and a half weeks but it felt a lot longer. Many of the games were one-sided. Australia: 869 for 1. Mozambique: 13 all out (including 8 wides). That sort of thing. Mozambique weren't really at the 2007 World Cup but they might well be at the next one.

Prices were high and often resulted in half-filled stadiums. The organisers seemed to think that the local West Indian population would happily hand over three months' wages to watch Scotland play the Netherlands. Money doesn't talk, it swears and the Caribbean air was full of expletives during this World Cup. As in spectators saying, ' $10 for a bottle of water? You must be f***ing joking!' The ICC measured the tournament by the amount of money it made and declared it a resounding success.

West Indian cricket has 100 years of tradition, culture and vibrant hospitality. Much of this was knocked on the head during the 2007 World Cup. There were draconian restrictions on the crowds. During the first half of the tournament, anyone seen enjoying themselves or making a noise was threatened with ejection from the ground. If you wore a T-shirt with the wrong logo on (i.e. one of the sponsor's competitors), you had to cover it up. The only drink spectators could bring into the ground was Pepsi (one of the sponsors). One spectator, who at the first warm-up game arrived with his own water, was told he could not enter the ground with his plastic bottle, especially with the cap on, as this was clearly a deadly weapon. Paramedics later carried him out suffering from dehydration because he could not afford to purchase water at the exorbitant price being charged inside the ground.

At around the same time that West Indian citizens were having their human rights trampled all over, the Chief Constable of Derbyshire was demonstrating his own concern for human rights. The Derbyshire Constabulary refused to release the photographs of two convicted murderers who had escaped from police custody on the grounds that it might infringe the Human Rights and Data Protection Act. Presumably the Chief Constable couldn't be disciplined for stupidity because that may have infringed his human rights. It's a funny old world isn't it?

During the Group stages, England had to play Canada. Would Canada struggle against England if we played them at ice hockey or moose racing? No. Did England struggle to beat Canada in their Group C match? Yes. England did manage to get through to the so-called 'Super Eight' stage but only played well in their last match when they knew they couldn't progress to the knockout phase. The tournament had a fitting end with a final of such farcical ineptitude that it turned what should have been a sporting showpiece into a laughing stock. And if that wasn't bad enough, Australia won.

Lest we forget, the World Cup followed closely after England's disastrous showing in Australia, so it had not been a good few months for English cricket followers. (Thank goodness we bagged the big one - the memorably named Commonwealth Bank trophy). Having won the Ashes so magnificently in 2005, we lost them at the earliest opportunity just 15 months later. There was something very familiar about the Ashes campaign in 2006/07: Lack of preparation for matches. The opening bowler's first ball going straight into the hands of second slip. The side's best batsman being asked which number he would like to bat. Bowlers seemingly unable to bowl either line or length. Unfounded optimism exposed every time the side took the field. Has the gap between village cricket and Test cricket ever been closer?

The 2006/07 Ashes tour threw up a number of interesting questions. Is there anything Richard Branson won't do for publicity? Why was Saj Mahmood playing Test cricket five years before he was ready? Did Cricket Australia really think it would work if they told 40,000 Australians, the Barmy Army and presumably the odd Mexican that if they waved during Test matches they would be ejected from the ground?

The most talked about question - why was Giles picked ahead of Panesar? - is easily explained. Duncan Fletcher liked bowlers who could 'bat a bit' and Giles had done the business for him in 2005. You want a coach to be focused, single minded and loyal to his players but only when he is right. If he is wrong then the same qualities tend to work against him.

The question most difficult to answer is why was Pietersen batting at No 5? This is one of the great imponderables of our time; along with why can't you get Longwave on car radios anymore and why didn't Graham Thorpe let Alex Tudor get his century against New Zealand in 1999? It was once said of Graeme Souness in his playing days that if he were a chocolate soldier he would eat himself. The same epithet could equally apply to Kevin Pietersen. He obviously thought that he was England's best batsman and most people agreed with him, so why, in a side with a fragile top order and a tail as long as Tony Blair's Best Friends Christmas card list, did he bat at No 5? Does Ponting bat at 5? Does Tendulkar go in at 5? Did Viv Richards? It was all very strange. Kevin Pietersen's innate modesty or Duncan Fletcher's intransigence are really the only two possible explanations.

Meanwhile, in the summer of 2007, I was approaching the Clifton Hampden match with some trepidation. Not to put too fine a point on it, the SOPs had let me down badly. Despite having six months' notice of the date, one announced that he had to go to Estonia for the weekend. Another said that he was going to Barcelona for a 'stag weekend' - not even his own. A

118

third one had joined the RAF and was on a training course and a fourth had injured a shoulder playing rugby.

It was rather worrying. I had always managed to put out eleven players except for one year when I had twelve. I had tried to finesse the selection by assuming that Clive would not turn up and of course, on that occasion he had. Clifton Hampden agreed to play twelve as well so everyone was happy in the end.

Having too many players was not a problem that I was likely to be confronted with in the latest match. I needed to cast my selection net a little wider. Viv was a friend who had a shared love of Bob Dylan. She once played 'Don't Think Twice, It's All Right' to me on her guitar. I told her that she could have done better but I didn't mind. She had a husband who played proper cricket. He even went to pre-season nets. Walking a careful line between a casual invitation and utter desperation, I managed to secure his services to play.

Most of my friends could probably best be described as middle aged, middle class, middle of the road anarchists. You could add in one or two disillusioned socialists and the odd closet Lib Dem. David, however, was different. Not only did he admit to voting Conservative, he was going to be a candidate for them at the next general election. On the credit side, he was good at chess, not bad at golf and was also a huge Dylan fan. More importantly, he had a son, Andrew, who played cricket to a decent standard. Thankfully, he wasn't going to Latvia or Peru that weekend and he agreed to turn out at Clifton Hampden.

An interest in cricket is challenged by a love of Bob Dylan as the predominant theme amongst my close acquaintances. The love ranges from 'infatuation' to 'just good friends'. To me his genius is self-evident. He is up there with Shakespeare, Beethoven and Stan Bowles. Yes, he had a dodgy period in the late '70s and early '80s, when he embraced Christianity rather too wholeheartedly but his catalogue of great songs is extraordinary. Some people say, what are his songs about? I would refer them to Dylan's reply when he was once asked the same question. 'Some of them are about three minutes, some of them are about five minutes, and some of them, believe it or not, are about eleven minutes'.

I still needed two more players to complete the team in 2007. With less than a fortnight to go, I was beginning to be seriously concerned when I got a phone call from Clive. He no longer turned out for the team but said that he would definitely be coming down for the Clifton Hampden weekend and that his accountant would like to play. This was a big surprise to me - first of all to get an unsolicited call from Clive to confirm his attendance at Clifton Hampden and secondly to discover that he had an accountant. I hadn't realised that he had enough money to buy a round let alone employ an accountant. All those years of cadging cigarettes and sleeping on people's floors had obviously paid off.

Clive went on to say that he had been talking to his next door neighbour about the match and he wanted to play as well. Did I need either of them? I was grateful and suspicious in equal measure, but beggars can't always be choosers so I said that, as it happens, I was a bit short this year and it would be great if they could both play. Clive agreed to speak to them and get back to me.

The week of the match arrived and I still hadn't heard

from Clive so I thought it prudent to ring him. The conversation went something like this:

Me: 'Hi Clive. How's it going?'
Clive: 'Great thanks. I'm looking forward to the weekend.'
Me (trying not to sound anxious): 'Yes, it should be good. Any luck with those two players?'
Clive: 'Oh yeah. I sent a text to my neighbour and I'm waiting to hear from him.'
Me: (trying not to sound petulant) 'If he's your next door neighbour couldn't you just pop round and see him?'
Clive: 'Well he's in Portugal.'
Me: 'Oh I see. When does he get back?'
Clive: 'On Friday I think. He's on a cricket tour.'

Even in the middle of an extreme anxiety attack with visions of turning up with only nine men (or less), I managed to feel impressed that one of my potential players was on an overseas cricket tour.

Me: 'Is he still OK to play on Sunday?'
Clive: 'He said he was up for it before he went away.'
Me: (trying to sound reassured) 'Oh jolly good.'
Clive: 'Do you still need Richard, my accountant?'
Me: 'Well yes, I was rather hoping he would play.'
Clive: 'I'll tell him he's definitely needed then.'
Me: 'Great. See you at the weekend.'

So, after more than 30 years, I was still relying on the

kindness of strangers to make up the team. The weekend arrived and sure enough so did Clive but there was no sign of his neighbour or his accountant. I asked him for news of his two players.

Clive: 'Richard said he will definitely be down tomorrow and will meet us in The Plough at lunchtime.'
Me: 'Is he reliable?'
Clive: 'Of course. He's an accountant.'
Me: 'Do you mean like those guys from Arthur Andersen who signed off the books at Enron?'
Clive: 'Just relax Mike. Have I ever let you down?'

No reply was really needed for that one so I asked about his neighbour.

Clive 'George got back from Portugal last night and he's aiming to bring his wife and kids down to the camp site later this afternoon, do a bit of fishing and then play on Sunday.'

Even at my most wildly optimistic, I could see that there were some potential pitfalls in this plan. Husband comes home from week-long cricket tour in Portugal and announces to wife that they are off with the kids for a weekend of camping, fishing and cricket. She would have to be a cross between Mother Teresa, Rachel Heyhoe-Flint and Ray Mears' sister to agree to that. Clive swept aside my doubts and once again told me to relax. Relax? This was the Clifton Hampden weekend, how was I supposed to relax?

Later that evening in the pub, I had the following conversation:

Clive: 'I've just had a call from George. His wife isn't too keen about coming down.'
Me: 'Fair enough but his wife isn't playing. What about him?'
Clive: 'The thing is, it's raining in London.'
Me: (with an almost overwhelming sense of déjà vu) 'Well it's not raining here.'
Clive: '.....and the forecast is bad for Sunday. George said he might try and come down on his own tomorrow if it clears up.'

There was nothing left to do but to go and buy Rob a pint and ask him if he had brought his cricket kit with him. He had and he confirmed that he was happy to play if I really needed him.

That night, in common with most of the country and most of the summer, it poured with rain. It looked like the game would be off, but the next morning the sun came out and, although a hard rain continued to fall over the rest of the country, Clifton Hampden had a beautiful day. We reconvened in the Plough at Sunday lunchtime and, before long, Richard the accountant arrived. Trying not to look surprised, I welcomed him and rather uncharitably said that as he was a friend of Clive I had been a bit worried he might not turn up. He smiled generously and said that he was looking forward to playing. Introducing his 14 year old son standing next to him, he said 'Eric would like to play as well if you're short.'

I glanced at Rob and genuinely couldn't tell whether it

was a look of relief or disappointment that crossed his face. Whatever he felt, Rob immediately volunteered to stand down and, with half an hour to go before the start, 14 year old Eric became the final member of the team.

Clifton Hampden batted first and we started well. Tight bowling and adequate fielding restricted their run rate. David's son, Andrew, showed that he had bowled before and early on had a very confident LBW appeal turned down. The general consensus from bowler, wicketkeeper and first slip was that the ball had been missing the off stump and would have also missed leg. At the end of the over, in my capacity as captain, I made a polite enquiry to the umpire about the decision. 'It was doing a bit too much' came the reply.

Great! On a pitch as slow as an hourly rate lawyer doing his summing up, we finally had a bowler who 'did too much' with the ball. The fortunate recipient of the LBW decision was their best batsman and went on to score 95. His batting partner at the time was Cox-Rogers junior. As he was only a young lad, I had suggested to the bowlers that we take it easy on him. By the time I had found out that he played for Oxfordshire under 15s, he was 20 not out and driving the ball effortlessly through the covers. In my defence, he did look younger than he was. At tea, we were confronted by an impressive total of 215.

Clive's accountant looked as though he knew how to bat so I asked him to open. He fell to the curse of the newcomer hoping to impress and was out for 0. His son Eric, batting at No 11, was also out for 0 so the scorebook had a balanced, double entry look about it. Thankfully, Viv's husband - also called Clive - scored some runs and John, my eldest son, once again showed that he doesn't really appreciate how difficult batting is by top scoring despite it being his first game of cricket for two years.

I found a new way of getting out at Clifton Hampden - run out by my son. I have to admit that I was 'ball watching' and at the time said it was 100% my fault. I have since revised this to 90% my fault. By the time I write the sequel to this book (working title: 'It's All Over Now, Baby Blue' - 50 years of the Clifton Hampden cricket match), it will probably be closer to 10% my fault.

The rest of the team didn't do much better. Cox-Rogers junior took 3 wickets with teenage leg spin that you are so determined not to get out to, that it guarantees that you do. We fell well short of the Clifton Hampden total. We had lost, again, but I felt it was important to take the long view. When Mao Tse-tung was asked what he thought the consequences of the French Revolution had been, he replied that it was too early to tell. There were still plenty of Clifton Hampden matches to come. I would continue to take the positives wherever I could find them.

13. Time Passes Slowly

You are on a three-hour Health & Safety training course. Or maybe sitting on a stationary train because, against all the odds, some leaves have fallen on the line in October. What do you do to pass the time? You make up cricket teams such as best all time England XI since the 2nd World War versus best Australian XI? All time World XI to play Mars? Players beginning with 'B' XI? Don't be ashamed, you are not alone. We've all done it at some time or other.

This is my eclectic eleven who did things a bit differently and I would love to see them play together in some parallel universe.

1. MARVAN ATAPATTU's middle name is Samson. Not a lot of people know that. Furthermore, he is one of only three

genuine Test batsmen to get a pair on their Test debut (Graham Gooch and Saeed Anwar are the others). Atapattu then scored 0 and 1 in his second Test and another pair in his third. So after six innings, and in the side for his batting, he had scored a solitary run and his batting average was 0.167. The Sri Lankan selectors perhaps could be forgiven for giving up on him. But they didn't; they gave him another chance and got their reward. Go on a few pages in Wisden and you find that only Bradman, Hammond and Lara have scored more double centuries than Atapattu in Test cricket. He went on to score 5,502 runs for Sri Lanka at an average of just over 39. He was also made captain but had to give it up when he was injured early in 2006. He was controversially left out of the 2007 World Cup team despite his huge experience of 268 ODI matches. When he was finally recalled in June 2007, he turned down the opportunity to play in the home Test series against Bangladesh. Consequently, he wasn't selected for the short tour of Australia but Sri Lanka's sports minister intervened and Atapattu was drafted into the squad. Clearly, he didn't get on with the Sri Lankan selectors in 2007 as well as he had when he made his debut in 1990. Atapattu memorably referred to them as 'muppets headed by a joker' during the first Test in Brisbane. Unsurprisingly, he announced his retirement after the second Test with plans to join the 'rebel' Indian Cricket League. He scored 80 in his final innings against Australia in what was his 90th Test match. Failure is truly the first step on the way to success; at least it was for Marvan Samson Atapattu.

2. NORMAN CALLAWAY scored a double century for New South Wales against Queensland at the Sydney Cricket Ground on his first class debut. It was February 1915 and he was not yet nineteen. It turned out to be his only first class innings. He joined the Australian Imperial Forces and was killed in France at the second Battle of Bullecourt during an attack on the Hindenberg Line in May 1917. No one can say how his career would have gone but it's safe to say that he would have been a pretty good player, maybe even a great one. In purely cricketing terms, Norman Callaway's death epitomises the waste and futility of the First World War. He did, however, achieve statistical cricket immortality. His 207 gives him the highest first class career batting average, assuming no innings qualifications, dwarfing Bradman's 95.14.

3. GEORGE HEADLEY was known as the 'black Bradman' in many places, except the West Indies where Bradman was referred to as the 'white Headley'. He was the first 'great' batsman to play for the West Indies. Yet only American bureaucracy stopped him being lost to baseball. He was due to go to America in 1927 and study dentistry but his visa was delayed. Instead, at the age of eighteen, he scored 211 for Jamaica against a strong English touring side led by the Hon. Lionel Tennyson and never left for the United States. During the ten years before the Second World War, he was called the 'Atlas' of West Indian cricket because he carried their batting on his shoulders. He was the first black man to captain the West Indies when he was made captain for

one Test in 1947. Apart from Bradman, only three batsmen have an average above 60 in Test matches - George Headley, Graeme Pollock, and Herbert Sutcliffe. George Headley was the first of three generations to play Test cricket. His son, Ron, played 2 Tests for the West Indies in 1973 and his grandson, Dean, played 15 Tests for England in the late 1990s'. There is only one other instance of three consecutive generations playing Test cricket and I'm sure that you really want to know what that was. Jahangir Khan played 4 Tests for India in the 1930s'. He was the father of Majid Khan, the exciting and charismatic batsman who played 63 Tests for Pakistan. Majid's son, Bazid, played for Pakistan once in 2004. For good measure, Majid's cousins - Imran Khan and Javed Burki - both captained Pakistan.

4. COLIN INGLEBY-MACKENZIE would be captain. He is famous for telling his Hampshire 1961 Championship winners to 'be in bed by breakfast time'. Despite the strength of Surrey and Yorkshire at the time, Hants won the Championship on a tidal wave of champagne, intuitive leadership and bold declarations. Ingleby had earlier captained E.W Swanton's XI to the West Indies in 1959. Worried about the team's erratic form, Swanton suggested a curfew. 'I'd like everyone in bed by 11, Colin.' 'Oh I don't know that's such a good idea Jim' replied Ingleby 'we start play at 11.30.' After this tour, Ingleby was due to begin a new job in the City on February 1st. He turned up on March 18th. He had been enjoying an extended Caribbean holiday too much to leave. Ingleby-Mackenzie was Hampshire's last amateur captain.

He once persuaded an umpire to bring a radio on to the pitch so he could listen to a horse race while he was fielding. His apparent indifference and easy-going manner disguised a determination to succeed, which he did with great style and daring. You can't ask for more than that.

5. GARY SOBERS is in the team because he was my first, and enduring, cricketing hero. He also happens to be the best all rounder that has ever played the game. The first test of a world-class all rounder is to ask whether he would get in the side for his batting if he didn't bowl or for his bowling if he couldn't bat. Sobers scored 8,032 runs in 93 Tests which puts him in the upper echelons of batsmen ever to play Test cricket. His average of 57.78 has only been exceeded by a handful of players. Yet he started his West Indian career at seventeen as an orthodox slow left arm bowler. Frank Worrell encouraged him to develop into a Test-class fast medium pace bowler. Sobers also cultivated his left arm wrist spin and he continued to bowl either fast or slow, as the match circumstances demanded, with equal control. Over his Test career, he took 235 wickets, which has only been surpassed by six West Indian bowlers. He was also a brilliant fielder and took 110 catches, mainly in the slips and short leg. His first century for the West Indies was 365 not out which remained the highest Test score for over 36 years. He was the first player to score six sixes in an over when, in 1968, playing for Nottinghamshire against Glamorgan, he demolished Malcolm Nash. (Shastri, playing for Bombay against Baroda, equalled the feat in 1984.)

Averages and statistics, of course, do not tell the whole story. Sobers had a grace and elegance which, when combined with a competitive nature and innate ability, made him so compelling to watch.

6. IAN BOTHAM announced his arrival to the cricket world at the age of eighteen when he had four teeth knocked out by a bouncer from Andy Roberts. Playing for Somerset against Hampshire in a Benson & Hedges quarterfinal, he continued batting, hitting two sixes in an innings of 45 not out, Somerset winning by one wicket. This set a marker for the heroics that followed. He first played for England in 1977 and for the next five years, dominated English cricket. He achieved the Test double of 1000 runs and 100 wickets in 21 Tests at the age of twenty three, both records that still stand today. Judged at the highest level, Botham wasn't a 'great' batsman such as Viv Richards or Len Hutton. He scored 5,200 runs at just over 33 in Tests but any cricket follower would stop what he or she was doing and watch when he went out to bat. Equally, he wasn't a 'great' bowler like Fred Trueman or Shane Warne, although he remains England's leading wicket taker with 383 wickets at 28.4 each. But he was undoubtedly a 'great' cricketer. He had a charisma given to very few. His batting was uninhibited whatever the circumstances and his bowling was imbued with self-belief. When Mike Brearley gave up the England captaincy, the selectors gambled and gave the position to Botham at the age of 24. He captained England for 12 Tests of which 4 were lost and 8 drawn. It was ill luck and unfortunate timing that most of them were

against the West Indies who were the dominant, not to say irresistible, force of the time. Botham was still captain at the start of the 1981 series against the Australians. England lost the first Test and then drew at Lords. Botham got a 'pair' and resigned from the captaincy before the selectors could sack him. Most players would have struggled to hit any sort of form after that but Botham has never been plagued by the curse of self-doubt. At Headingley, he took 6 for 95 in the Australian first innings and scored 50 when England batted. His epic 149 not out in the second innings, when England followed on, helped set the Australians 130 to win and they were bowled out for 111. Rather less well known is the Fourth Test at Edgbaston when Australia only needed 151 to win. Botham took the last five wickets, with figures of 14 overs, 9 maidens, 5 for 11, and they were all out for 121. At Old Trafford in the next Test, Botham came in at 104 for 5 and scored an extraordinary 118, which included six sixes and thirteen fours. England won again and Botham was named man of the match for the third game in a row. This series established his legendary status but he played Test cricket for another 10 years and was never less than entertaining.

7.   SAMUEL BECKETT as well as being able to write a bit, was a natural athlete. He excelled at cricket as a left handed batsman and left arm medium pace bowler. He played two first-class games for Dublin University against Northamptonshire. As a result, he became the only Nobel Prize winner to have an entry in Wisden. (Another good pub cricketing question!)

Beckett is probably best known for his play 'Waiting for Godot'. The critic Vivian Mercier wrote in the Irish Times that Beckett 'has achieved a theoretical impossibility - a play in which nothing happens, yet keeps audiences glued to their seats. What's more, since the second act is a subtly different reprise of the first, he has written a play in which nothing happens, twice.' Some may find the resemblance to cricket irresistible. Beckett loved cricket passionately. He was once walking with a friend towards Lords on a glorious summer morning, to watch England bat in a Test Match. His friend, in a joyful mood, turned to Beckett and said 'Makes you feel it's good to be alive, doesn't it?' There was a slight pause before Beckett replied, ' I wouldn't go quite as far as to say that.'

8. OSSIE COLHOUN would be the wicket keeper. His greatest moment came in 1969 when he kept wicket for Ireland against the West Indies on the famous occasion when Ireland dismissed the side that had just drawn the Second Test at Lord's, for 25. This result was completely unrelated to the trip arranged for the West Indies party to the Guinness brewery the day before. Ossie was also Ireland's night watchman for many years. One time in this role, playing at Perth (Scotland not Australia), he was run out going for a third run! This remarkable act of eccentric brilliance was matched by Robin Marlar who was once stumped second ball for 6, going in as night watchman for Sussex.

9. SYDNEY BARNES, better known as SF Barnes, was arguably
    the best bowler ever to play cricket. Comparing players
    when their careers just miss is difficult - Lillee or Trueman?
    Or overlap - McGrath or Ambrose? Or even in the same
    team - Marshall or Holding? So trying to compare Barnes,
    whose professional career started in 1895 and finished
    in 1938, with all the bowlers in history is more or less
    impossible. What is indisputable is that he took the most
    number of wickets in a Test series. On the 1913-14 tour
    to South Africa, he took 49 wickets in just four Tests at an
    average of less than 11. To put this in context, only two
    players in the history of cricket - Laker (46 wickets) and
    Grimmett (44 wickets) - have got more than 40 wickets in a
    five match Test series, Barnes did not play in the fifth Test
    because of a contractual dispute. He was a singular man
    who stood up for what he thought was right. In his second
    Test match ever, against Australia in 1901 at Melbourne, he
    had the extraordinary figures of 11 overs, 7 maidens, 6 runs,
    5 wickets. This is how Charlie Macartney, described the ball
    that clean bowled Victor Trumper in the first Test. 'The
    ball was fast on the leg stump but just before it pitched it
    swung suddenly to the off. Then it pitched, broke back and
    took Vic's leg stump. It was the sort of ball a man might see
    if he was dreaming or drunk.' This was from an Australian
    batsman standing at the bowler's end! Sydney Barnes was
    a right arm fast medium bowler with the accuracy, spin
    and variation of a slow bowler. Rather like Shane Warne
    bowling at Glenn McGrath's pace. For much of the time he
    was England's best bowler, he played his domestic cricket in

the Lancashire Leagues and for Staffordshire in the Minor Counties' championship, in which competitions he took over 5,000 wickets at an average of less than 8 runs each. It seems incredible today but he played only a handful of county games for Warwickshire and Lancashire because he could never get the financial contract he felt he needed. He played for England on and off between 1901 and 1914, taking 189 wickets at 16.43. In 1929, at the age of 56, he took eight for 41, playing for the Minor Counties against the touring South Africans. SF Barnes was a phenomenon and would have troubled any batsman in any generation.

10. JIM LAKER was the greatest off spinner of all time. Born in Bradford but started playing for Surrey after the 2nd World War as Yorkshire were not interested in employing him. His 8 for 2 in 14 overs, in the 1950 Test Trial on a rain-damaged track at Bradford, must have given him great satisfaction. This was just a taster for what was to come. There are so many Test matches these days that most records will be broken at some point. However, it is reasonable to assume that Laker's 19-90 against the Australians in 1956 will never be bettered. The match took place at Old Trafford; Laker took 9-37 in the first innings and 10-53 in the second. Looking at the black and white film clips from the match, it is clear that the Australians were mesmerised and had no idea how to play him. Also remarkable were the restrained celebrations even when Laker got his 19th wicket. Nowadays, when every wicket is greeted with 'high fives' and 'group hugs' it is really rather refreshing to see. In all, Laker took

46 wickets at 9.6 each in the Test series. He also took 10-88 in an innings for Surrey against the Australians at the Oval later in the summer, finishing the season with an amazing 63 Australian wickets.

11. DEVON MALCOLM is a legend for a number of reasons. For a start, he was referred to as Malcolm Devon by Ted Dexter. An easy mistake to make you might think except that Dexter was Chairman of the selectors at the time. He was a genuinely quick bowler and that coupled with his bad eyesight, poor fielding and eccentric batting, made him someone to cherish in the charisma free zone of English cricket in the 1990s. He was a natural No. 11 batsman and usually batted like one but did once hit two successive sixes off Shane Warne. His place among the legends was assured when England played South Africa at the Oval in 1994. He was hit on the helmet first ball by a bouncer while batting against Fanie de Villiers. This rather upset Devon who reputedly said to the South African fielders 'you guys are history'. He did indeed take his revenge, ripping through the South African batting in the second innings to finish with figures of 9-57. It was the best bowling analysis, in Test cricket, by an English fast bowler in the 20th Century.

12th man and scorer would be The Revd. J.C.Crawford who was the only objector to a 1902 MCC motion that the bowling crease be increased from 78 inches to 80 inches but refused to give his reason to the Chairman[6].

---

6   Source: 'Carr's Dictionary of extra-ordinary English Cricketers' by J.L. Carr.

So, Devon Malcolm and Sydney Barnes open the bowling. If Devon was having one of his off days, Ian Botham would come on as first change. If you could get the ball away from Barnes, then perhaps Samuel Beckett would turn his arm over for a few overs. Jim Laker and Gary Sobers would then finish the opposition off. I would expect Atapattu, Callaway and Headley to score at least 200 between them. Then, after a brief cameo from Ingleby-Mackenzie, sit back and enjoy Sobers and Botham batting together. The rest of the team could all bat a bit so anything under 500 would be a disappointment. The variety and quality of the bowling attack would surely secure victory by an innings.

14. Forever Young

Some might think that a more appropriate title for the last chapter would be 'Knocking on Heaven's Door' but I prefer the more optimistic 'Forever Young'. Cricket does help to keep you young, in heart and mind if not always in body. Football may be the mistress that you have fun with from time to time but cricket is the wife you love forever. If you had to choose between the two, you would always choose cricket. I hasten to add that this is simply a metaphor and on no account should be taken literally.

Cricket is such a wonderful game. As the great Warwickshire all rounder, William Shakespeare, said; 'age cannot wither her, nor custom stale her infinite variety'. What other activity can teenage boys and middle aged men join in together without the latter either being arrested or having a heart attack?

Life is like a cricket match. Long periods where nothing seems to be happening and then all of a sudden some excitement. Like life, it's good to win but it's the taking part that really counts. You want to avoid total humiliation like being Simon Dee or Mark Thatcher. The difference is that once you are Mark Thatcher then that's it, you are Mark Thatcher for life and there's not a lot you can do about it. But in cricket, if you are destroyed at Lords in the First Test, you can still come back and win the Ashes. If you are all out for 32 one year, you can come back and (eventually) win four matches in a row.

For many people, England's Ashes win was a memorable highlight of 2005. For me there was something else that almost matched it that year. I spotted a mistake in Wisden! On page 271, only three players are listed as having achieved the Test treble of 1000 runs, 100 wickets and 100 catches. Gary Sobers, Ian Botham and, rather more surprisingly, Carl Hooper. A few pages later, Shane Warne is listed as one of the 21 players to have got 100 catches in Test cricket. Well clearly he had 100 wickets and he's also got more than 1000 runs. It was my duty to contact Wisden immediately.

I had this delightful email in response:

Hi Mike

Thanks for your email: you're not the first to point out our omission, but it doesn't diminish the value of what you say.

I've just double-checked - and we do include Warne in the list of those to have taken the all-rounders' treble in Wisden 2006.

Thanks again for taking the trouble to write to us - and with best wishes.

Hugh Chevallier
Deputy Editor
Wisden Cricketers' Almanack

I don't want to give the impression that I spend all my time reading Wisden. I also play as much cricket as my body will allow, talk about cricket quite a bit, watch a lot of cricket on TV thanks to Sky, go to the occasional Test match and play in the back garden or on the beach whenever I can persuade my sons or friends to join me. So I think you will agree that is a pretty full and rounded life.

Half our team at the Clifton Hampden match these days think that there has been nothing decent on the radio since 'Round the Horne', that Alan Hudson is the best Chelsea midfielder of recent times and that Flintoff may be the new Botham. The other half don't listen to the radio because they've all got ipods, will only become aware of Alan Hudson when they read his obituary and think that Botham was the old Flintoff.

Colin, Roger and I are still trying to work out what to do with our lives but at least we know what we are going to be doing one weekend every year. In a changing world, it is reassuring to know that the Clifton Hampden match is always there. People ask (in desperation sometimes) how long will it keep going? My own rule, hitherto kept a secret, is that I want to keep playing until my batting average exceeds my bowling average. Since this is never going to happen, it seems that the Clifton Hampden match will go on in perpetuity. For younger readers, this is not a small village in France. It just means that the Clifton Hampden match will go on and on and on and on and on.

Dramatis Personae

Mike Harfield The captain, so always gets picked. Author, husband, father, cricketer, man of many parts - some of them still working.

Steve Knowles Our only Kolpak player, based in Munich. Steve, born and bred in Leeds, has been known as Herman the German by two generations of opposition teams.

Colin Day A man with a startlingly small epiglottis. Painfully slow drinker, even slower bowler. A class warrior on a generous final salary pension scheme.

Mike Davies Typical Yorkshireman. Calm, philosophical in defeat, laughs when he is run out, jokes with the opposition when he is hit for a boundary.

Ray Bamford aka 'Reg', struggled against the moving ball so took up golf.

Nick Cullum Sometimes known as 'One shot' Cullum because of his table football style. The sobriquet could equally be attributed to his batting style, or indeed many other aspects of his life.

Roger Kay Taught the law and the law won. Now a Professor. Top score of 49 at Clifton Hampden. Still in therapy.

Roger Walworth	Continues to play a straight bat when all around him are falling. Sold his sports shops so that he could play more golf.
Rob McKeith	Born under a bad sign. Rob developed the low full-toss years before it became de rigueur in one day cricket.
Hugh Parry	Intellectually gifted, sartorially challenged. No one who saw his Rupert Bear trousers has ever forgotten or forgiven.
Clive Fenner	Had an audition as a drummer for Dire Straits, but didn't turn up because he didn't think a band with that name could succeed. Very bad judge of a run as well.
Richard Bamford	First of the SOPs to play at Clifton Hampden. Represented his Cambridge college..........at rowing.
Richard Kay	Another SOP regular. Lawyer, son of two lawyers, future father of a lawyer. Mystifyingly slow between the wickets.
Bob Chappell	Lives in South Africa now, but still dreams of one more appearance. A fearless, if unconventional, fielder.
Vernon Meade	If you read this Vernon, the bar is always open, please come back!

John Shaw	A regular for a few years and then went off to train as a 'mature' doctor. (Can you train as an 'immature' doctor? The evidence would suggest that you can.)
John Harfield	Heir apparent but has moved to Edinburgh. Oh dear.
Duncan McNab	Has also moved to Edinburgh but has more excuse.
Colin Walters	Used a lot of bottom hand (not a euphemism), scored a century and then buggered off. Come back Colin, we need you!
Alastair Walworth	Coached by Derek Randall, went to Bedford School, first name Alastair, last name, alas, not Cook.
John Broadfoot	As reliable as Elizabeth Taylor's wedding vows or Jeffrey Archer's CV.
James Davies	A high flying SOP. (aeroplanes not drugs)
David Harfield	Will play if required but I won't be leaving my Wisdens to him.
Jack Broadfoot	Another trainee doctor, which could come in useful in future matches.
Mike Hughes	Played a couple of games in the '80s. Good bat.
Jake Nash	Local conscript recruited from Clifton Hampden at the 11th hour (twice).

Mark Whittingham	Got married, moved to Newcastle, had a baby.......availability now limited.
Stuart Chambers	Made one appearance and then left to become Chief Executive of Pilkington. (If you read this Stuart, we're looking for a tour sponsor.)
John Forest	Friend of a friend. Played in the first match. Wore sandals when batting.
Chris Martin	Another friend of a friend. Might have been picked more often if he had brought Gwyneth along.
Craig Middlemass-Spencer	Very long name so no room to say anything about him.
Andrew Mowat	Yet another trainee doctor, but at Oxford so no excuse on future availability.
Tony Newman	A single appearance from an Australian, just to show there's no prejudice.
Les Poulton	A visitor from Munich in the early days, so long ago he may well have been on the same plane as Neville Chamberlain.
Tim Raydon	Scored an elegant 50, went to darkest Africa and was never heard of again.
Alan Ross	Good hockey player. Very attractive girlfriend.

Chris Schwarck	Another local Clifton Hampden recruit. Dislocated his shoulder hitting a boundary in one of our many unsuccessful run chases.
Paul Squires	Came all the way up from Devon and didn't get a bat. If it wasn't for bad luck, he wouldn't have no luck at all.
Eric Thistle	The only SOP to make his debut in the same game as his father.
Richard Thistle	Clive's accountant. Manages his offshore accounts on the Isle of Dogs.
Bob Vaughan	I told Bob that he should try everything once, except incest and folk dancing, so he agreed to play. He didn't bat and didn't bowl but saved the game in 1999.
Tom Warburton	Gave the captain out LBW and never played again.
Clive Whittaker	2007 saw the first of many appearances, hopefully.

Tim Harfield came on as substitute in 2004 for an indisposed Mike Davies. Full debut expected any year now.

Acknowledgements

Clifton Hampden Cricket Club who made it all possible.

Dave Bowden and Jean Drew who both averaged nearly 100 every Clifton Hampden match (pints pulled and sandwiches made).

The 42 players who have turned out for the Mike Harfield XI over the years; it wouldn't have been the same without you.

Robert Zimmerman for his song titles, and his songs.

Thanks to Viv for her help - I still can't remember all the best things she said.

Cover design by John Harfield and Vivyan Whittaker.

In 1994, Colin Walters scored 113 for us. It is the only century scored by either side in the 30 year Clifton Hampden series. We still lost.

Gary Sobers now prefers to be known as Garry rather than Gary. I can't get used to this, it just doesn't look right, so I have continued to refer to him as Gary Sobers throughout this book and probably always will.

Arthur Cunynghame for his help and encouragement, and for his chance meeting with Tony Mills in Waterstone's Macclesfield.